The Neurotic Woman

The Neurotic Woman
The Role of Gender in Psychiatric Illness

Agnes Miles

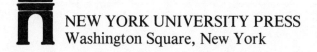

NEW YORK UNIVERSITY PRESS
Washington Square, New York

First published in the USA in 1988 by
NEW YORK UNIVERSITY PRESS
Washington Square,
New York, NY 10003

Library of Congress Cataloging-in-Publication Data

Miles, Agnes
  The neurotic woman.

  Bibliography: p.
  Includes index.
  1. Women—Mental health.   2. Neuroses—Social
aspects.   I. Title.
RC451.4.W6M55   1988   616.85'2'0088042   87-35682
ISBN 0-8147-5441-4

Typeset in 11pt Times Roman by
Quality Phototypesetting Ltd., Bristol

Printed in Great Britain by
Billings & Sons Ltd, Worcester

$15.00

Contents

List of Tables

Acknowledgements

The research on which this book is based was made possible by a grant from the University of Southampton Advanced Studies Committee.

Dr Penelope Tomlinson made a most valuable contribution to the field work.

1 Sociological Approaches to the Study of Neurosis

INTRODUCTION

Traditionally, sociologists were reluctant to study the social situation and experiences of people diagnosed as suffering from neurosis, just as they were reluctant to study the lives of sick people generally. In a widely read and influential book of the early 1970s, Eliot Freidson tried to account for the curious avoidance of sick people as a subject of study, by early sociologists. He referred to the enormous prestige and authority of medicine in Western societies; sociologists, like other non-medical 'laymen', believed the doctors who asserted that illness and the illness experience could be understood only by themselves. Sociologists held the medical conceptions of illness to be so authoritative, almost acquiring some 'special sanctity', that they considered the whole field of illness to be 'ruled out of sociology's purview' (Freidson, 1970).

More narrowly, the study of neurosis was regarded as the province of psychologists and psychiatrists. Concepts of neurosis and explanations of neurotic behaviour in terms of psychoanalytic, and later cognitive and biological theories, dominated the field of study. Sociologists, if they thought about neurosis at all, believed that it could not be studied, let alone explained, without reference to prevalent psychological theories.

The predominance of psychologists and psychiatrists in the field of mental health studies was challenged, during the 1960s, by critics (some psychiatrists among them) who questioned the validity and usefulness of the concept of 'mental disorder'.

Sociologists began to demonstrate that certain of the experiences of people called mentally ill can usefully be analysed by sociological tools (for example the lives of patients in mental hospitals by Goffman, 1961 and Stanton and Schwartz, 1954), whilst others developed the argument that medical categories and indeed the very notions of illness and disease can be viewed as social constructs.

More recently. several important contributions towards a sociology of mental illness have come from researchers, not all of them sociologists, pursuing different goals and relying on a number of theoretical perspectives. The causes, treatment and outcome of various forms of mental illness have been investigated along with the experience of sufferers and the social consequence of becoming mentally ill. Investigators have included feminist sociologists, their interest aroused by evidence that rates of mental illness are consistently higher for women than for men. Some writers have sought to attribute this gender imbalance to the disadvantaged social position of women, to differences in the health and illness behaviour of the sexes and to the dissimilar treatment accorded to them by (mostly male) health professionals.

Gender differences are particularly marked in the rates of neurotic disorders. Epidemiological studies consistently show that far more women than men are diagnosed as suffering from these disorders (Weissman and Klerman, 1977). Indeed, the social stereotype of a 'neurotic' is a woman.

This book is concerned with people diagnosed as suffering from a neurotic disorder. The term 'neurosis' or 'neurotic disorder' is defined by the *Glossary of Mental Disorders,* recommended by the Royal College of Psychiatrists to the medical profession (Wyeth, 1980) as 'mental disorders without any demonstrable organic basis in which the patient may have considerable insight and has unimpaired reality testing in that he usually does not confuse his morbid subjective experiences and fantasies with external reality'. According to the glossary, the category 'Neurotic Disorders' includes the following sub-categories: Hysteria, Phobic States, Obsessive-compulsive Disorders, Neurotic Depression and Others.

In this book a sociological perspective is applied to neurotic illness, and the experiences of individuals will be described from that perspective. It is pertinent first to review some of the sociological approaches to the study of neurosis.

THE SOCIAL CAUSATION APPROACH

During the past twenty years or so much sociological attention has been directed to the possibility of certain illness conditions having social causes. Research in this field has gained impetus from a shift in medical thinking towards multicausal aetiology, i.e. the notion that a single disease can have, and indeed is likely to have, more than one cause. The part played by economic, cultural and social factors has been studied and there is now available an ever-increasing pool of causal variables for consideration if a better understanding of disease causation is to be achieved.

In the area of neurotic disorders, depression has received the most attention by sociologists, partly because it is more frequently diagnosed than any other neurotic condition and partly for the reason that depression can be seen as a peculiarly 'social' illness. George Brown, a leading researcher, putting forward a personal view, said

I believe that depression is essentially a social phenomenon. I would not make the same claim for schizophrenia though its onset and course are also greatly influenced by social factors. Society and depression are more fundamentally linked. I can envisage societies where depression is absent and others where the majority suffer from depression. (Brown, 1984)

In their influential study of depression in women, conducted in London in the 1970s, Brown and his colleagues identified a number of social factors which contributed to depression and which they divided between 'provoking agents' which determined when depression occurred (i.e. triggered the onset of the illness) and 'vulnerability factors' which made women more susceptible to depression (Brown and Harris, 1978). Among the provoking agents found to be important in depression were certain kinds of severe adverse events in the life of an individual such as the death of a close relative, a serious illness or car accident, the breakdown of a marriage etc; these events were carefully rated and their meaning for the woman concerned closely studied. It was found that events rated as 'severe' were almost four times more common among women suffering from depression than among 'normal' women in a control group. The researchers also discovered a number of ongoing difficulties such as poor housing, the threat of eviction for non-payment of rent, and drug-taking in the family, which acted as provoking agents.

With regard to vulnerability factors the researchers found that women who enjoyed close, confiding relationships, whether with husband, relative or friend, were less vulnerable to depression than those who did not have such supportive relationships. The loss of a mother before the age of eleven, lack of employment outside the home and the fact of being at home with young children (especially those under six years of age) were factors rendering women vulnerable to depression.

In another research project, Brown and a team of sociologists compared women living in an inner city and those in a small island community in the Outer Hebrides (Brown *et al.,* 1977). The researchers attempted to link the kind of neurotic condition which was most widespread in each community to the particular culture thereof. They found less depression but a greater prevalence of anxiety and obsessional states in the island; they suggested that a strong community gives much more support to its members, reducing their vulnerability to depression but that, conversely, vulnerability to anxiety is increased, in close communities, by the 'oppressive and even persecutory nature of that closeness' (p. 374).

In Australia, Scott Henderson led a multi-disciplinary team which investigated the possibility of a causal connection between neurosis and a lack of social support by relatives, friends, neighbours etc (i.e. social network). (Henderson *et al.,* 1978). The theme underlying their research is that human beings live in groups and that the ability to form bonds and the availability of people with whom to do so is of the utmost importance to the emotional well-being of individuals. In some of his writings Scott Henderson touches on the possibility that the group was so overwhelmingly important to the survival of early man that the capacity to form enduring bonds, in order to maximise satisfactory group life, gradually increased by selective mating. From this perspective there can be postulated an association between the mental health of individuals and the extent of their success in forming social relationships. Scott Henderson's research found that people suffering from neuroses tended to have smaller networks and less social support than did the members of a control group.

Although it is possible that neurotics have fewer and less satisfactory relationships than others exactly because they are neurotic (i.e. that neurotic illness reduces the acceptability of its sufferers as companions and reduces their capacity to seek out others) there is some evidence of lack of social support preceding the onset of neurosis, rather than being consequential to that condition.

THE LABELLING PERSPECTIVE

While the search for social factors in the causation of neurotic disorders continues, a very different approach to the study of mental illness—the labelling perspective—has gained adherents. This approach built on the theoretical foundations of the labelling perspective to deviance which was stated most clearly by Howard Becker (1963). He argued that what is called deviance in a society is an act of breaking society's rules; it does not exist independently of social rules. Thus, the mechanism of rule-making and the perception of certain actions as rule-breaking are as important for the sociologists who study deviance as the behaviour and characteristics of the deviants and the reasons for their so becoming. In other words, both those who are labelled deviant and those who label them should receive attention in studies of deviance.

The most systematic early application of this perspective to mental illness was made by Thomas Scheff (1966) who noted that the behaviour of many psychiatric patients can be regarded as 'rule-breaking' behaviour. According to Scheff, mental disturbance may arise from many diverse causes (biological, genetic, psychological) or may be due to stress. Some sufferers, but not all, become labelled mentally ill, and Scheff argued that the act of being so labelled is the most important thing that happens to the individuals concerned. Many writers since Scheff have applied the labelling perspective to a variety of illnesses. As far as neurosis is concerned, from the perspective of labelling the important issue is to determine how a person becomes labelled neurotic, and the important task for sociologists is to explore the processes of labelling and the motivation of those who label a person neurotic (the doctor, the family, etc.). The more moderate adherents to this approach do not deny the existence of neurosis, nor the importance of discovering its causes; but agree that processes of labelling are equally important.

There is a more extreme form of this labelling approach, however: some writers argue that the motivation and characteristics of deviants are unimportant in producing deviance and that it is the action of labelling that creates this. Most proponents of the labelling perspective of deviance have now discarded this extreme version but in the field of mental illness it is still prevalent among the more severe critics of the psychiatric enterprise. Such critics argue that the very existence of mental illness, and of neurosis within it, is questionable and that instead of searching for causes and treatment it would be better to discard the concept. They hold that the task for researchers should be to ask whose interests are served by inventing such notions as neurosis and to question the motivation of those who apply this label to individuals. For example, Garth Wood, in *The Myth of Neurosis,* (1983) argues that

for many thousands of years the human race has done without this concept of neurosis and must and will learn to do so again. That we have a word for it does not explain what it is, if it exists or what, if it truly exists, is the best thing to do about it. The concept of 'neurosis' has not helped the plight of 'neurotics'. (p. 48)

In this framework the very existence of neurosis is problematic, and neurotics are simply individuals so labelled by psychiatrists. It is not claimed that such individuals have no real difficulties and do not suffer, only that their problems do not constitute an illness which requires treatment. Moreover, Wood and like-minded others do not claim that no one among those diagnosed as mentally ill is really ill, only that many of them are not. Indeed, Wood makes a distinction between 'genuine psychiatric illness' and those which are 'considered today within the rightful province of psychiatry' but are not 'true' mental illnesses. In his view most individuals diagnosed as neurotic belong to the latter category.

As for the question as to why people are diagnosed as suffering from non-existent illnesses, it can be argued that it is in the interest of experts offering a treatment to insist that the condition they wish to treat really exists. This argument is also voiced by many critics of the trend to expand the boundaries of medicine.

THE MEDICALISATION OF UNHAPPINESS

A number of sociologists have commented on the trend in Western societies whereby ever more social and emotional problems are interpreted within a medical, particularly psychiatric, framework. Probably, this does no more than reflect the rising expectation of people generally that all human problems should be amenable to solution through the services of one or another relevant professional (Zola, 1972).

People increasingly turn to doctors with their problems, thus stretching the boundaries of medical care. There has been a proliferation of medical helpers whose job it is to assist, advise and control and some would have it that their very presence in such numbers fuels the demand for their services.

Critics of the concept of 'neurotic disorder' contend that by applying this diagnosis to people with troubles, unhappiness becomes medicalised. It is of interest to consider why so many people take to their doctor problems which others accept as 'part of life' and why doctors think that these problems are proper subjects for their professional skills.

For many people, opportunities to seek help or advice are no longer readily to hand. In many areas the old cohesiveness of community life has given way in the face of increased mobility, and men and women can find themselves living in 'commuter country' perhaps far from the relatives and long-established friends and neighbours to whom they could formerly turn. Others are re-housed into estates and tower-blocks and hardly know anyone around them. Fewer people consult the parish priest, while newer professional advice-givers, such as social workers or family counsellors, are not always easy to find or are available only through a doctor's referral. General practitioners, on the other hand, are always available for consultation, which can be one reason why people take their troubles to them; another is that medical problems are more socially acceptable than personal ones. Problems that cause much unhappiness, such as failure in marriage, in career or as parents, excess drinking, or drug addiction may carry an imputation of personal blame; a medical explanation renders the individual blameless. It is more acceptable to be thought ill than to be thought inadequate and a failure. Yet another reason for turning to doctors is that they can prescribe pills which, although they do not solve problems, at least give temporary relief. To be able to sleep, to have one's anxiety or depression lifted, albeit temporarily, is very desirable.

Is it true that doctors, in turn, are willing to medicalise unhappiness by giving it a medical label and by issuing prescriptions to people whose complaints appear to have no recognisable medical basis?

There was certainly a large increase in the number of tranquillisers and other psychotropic drugs used during the 1960s and 1970s in the UK and other Western countries. Indeed, in the United States of America the tranquilliser valium became the most frequently prescribed drug (OHE, 1975; Cooperstock, 1978; Koumjian, 1981). Although some decrease was noted in the early 1980s (Koumjian, 1981; Hemminki *et al.,* 1981) the level of tranquilliser prescription is still historically high. Garth Wood argues that there is much pressure on psychiatrists to provide treatment for unhappiness:

If somebody presents himself for 'help', throws himself on our mercy, then we feel we should bend over backwards to provide it. It makes us feel better if we do, worse if we don't . . . . Thus the sufferers from the problems of life, served up to the psychiatrists by the impotent GPs, are often taken on in the out-patients department for periodic sessions of reassurance and support, and given trial courses of various pills'. (Wood, 1983, p. 30)

It can certainly be argued that doctors are committed, by their training and medical values, to helping patients. When a patient complains of emotional or social problems, which perhaps cause sleepless nights, loss of appetite or feelings of depression, the doctor may well prefer prescribing a medicine to turning away the patient unaided.

It has been noted that psychiatrists increasingly accept for treatment patients with a whole range of 'socio-behavioural' problems (Richman and Barry, 1985). But there is also pressure on general practitioners and psychiatrists to assign the patients they treat to a diagnostic category: the patient must be assumed to suffer from a medical condition if treatment is given. There is no medical condition called unhappiness or socio-behavioural problem, and the category that doctors can easily make use of is that of neurotic disorders. 'Depression', 'anxiety' or simply 'neurosis' can all be used to explain the prescription of a minor tranquilliser or sedative and thus become what Wood and Scheff call the 'dustbin' category of medical diagnosis.

General practitioners and psychiatrists may also undertake to provide treatment for people with 'problems of life' but no mental illness, because of the increased emphasis on prevention. In general, the limits of medicine are expanding, as doctors attempt to reach healthy but vulnerable individuals in order to prevent the onset of disease. In the particular area of mental health, Richman and Barry (1985) argue that psychiatrists take on patients with less serious emotional problems than they did in the past, aiming to forestall breakdown.

Clearly there are pressures on general practitioners and psychiatrists to medicalise 'unhappiness' but critics point to the possibility of another, ulterior motive, namely the widening of practioners' opportunities and spheres of influence. A profession may wish to expand into new areas in order to gain more power, and having moved into the field of 'treating unhappiness' may be reluctant to leave it in spite of lack of success. Wood argues that

no group of people, professional or otherwise, is keen to lose control over areas which they have previously widely considered their sovereign territory. That is human nature. There is the implication that their usefulness may be somewhat reduced in the process, indispensability compromised, and at the end of the day job security threatened. (1983, p. 29)

Be that as it may, it should be remembered that the area of

medical care expands according to the demand for it, even if the reverse is true also.

So far, the social causation and labelling approaches have been considered, but it should be noted that these are not mutually exclusive alternatives. It is possible that neurotic disorders contribute a meaningful medical psychological entity, the causes of which can usefully be studied, while at the same time it is possible that certain individuals are labelled neurotic for reasons best revealed by studies of their labellers.

THE PERSPECTIVE OF FEMINIST SOCIOLOGISTS

The female preponderance in rates of neurotic disorders was mentioned before. Studies in many Western countries have shown that far more women than men are diagnosed as suffering from neurosis; this gender differential is true of community samples, patients of general practitioners and psychiatric clinics, and admissions to mental hospitals (for a review, see Weissman and Klerman, 1977). Feminist sociologists have become interested in this greater susceptibility of women to neurosis, and as well as examining previous findings have conducted fresh research in an attempt to offer explanations from a feminist perspective. In their studies they have made use of both the social causation and labelling approaches to neurosis.

Several feminist sociologists favour the argument that neurotic disorders are real and indeed lead to much suffering in women. For example, Penfold and Walker (1984) maintain that depression 'although ill defined and misunderstood, is no myth' (p. 174). The feminist argument is that women become depressed because they have reasons to be so; that their position in society is one of disadvantage vis-à-vis that of men. Indeed sociologists have documented that women's education, employment, power, prestige and opportunities compare unfavourably with corresponding aspects of the male situation (Doyal, 1979; Garmanikov *et al.,* 1983A; Garmanikov *et al.,* 1983B). Research, not primarily into the causes of depression but intent on portraying the nature of women's lives within the social structure of contemporary Western societies, has identified domestic work, looking after and caring for aged, infirm or disabled relatives, among many unsatisfactory and, indeed, stressful features of the situation of women (Oakley, 1974; Rosenberg, 1984; Graham, 1984). If depression is a female condition (as statistics show), there must be a very real possibility that it is rooted in these and other disadvantageous aspects of the female role, a supposition confirmed by the work of Brown and Harris (1978).

A recent sociological work on agorophobia indicates that this too is a real problem, not a myth, and that, like depression, it is linked to the particular stresses experienced by married women who are engaged full-time on domestic duties (Brown, 1986). Sociological studies of other phobias, and of anxiety and obsessional states, are largely lacking.

Thus, from a causation approach, feminist writers link certain features of the social structure to causes of neurotic disorders in women and explain female preponderance in rates of neurosis by pointing to women's disadvantaged position. From a labelling approach, depression and other neurotic disorders are regarded by feminist writers as psychiatric labels which hide the essentially social nature of women's problems. For example, Ann Oakley and Paula Nicolson question the validity and usefulness of the notion of 'post-natal depression' (Oakley, 1981B; Nicolson, 1986). They argue that by setting up this category doctors medicalise the unhappiness following childbirth experienced by some women. Several feminist researchers focus attention on the labellers and their motivation for labelling women; amongst these are sociologists who have studied the prescriptions for tranquillisers and anti-depressants issued to women by general practitioners and psychiatrists.

It has been amply documented that far more women than men receive prescriptions for psychotropic drugs. For example, in a Canadian survey by Choiton *et al.* (1976) it was found that the use of tranquillisers and sedatives was 2.2 times more frequent among women; elsewhere it was shown that two-thirds of such prescriptions went to women (Hemminki, 1974). In another Canadian study, of valium users, Cooperstock and Lennard (1979) found that the underlying reason of doctors for prescribing valium for women on a prolonged basis was to maintain them 'in a role which they found difficult or intolerable without the drug'. The role which the drugs enabled women to continue in was the domestic role. Likewise, Barrett and Roberts (1978) found that British doctors aimed to 'readjust' their middle-aged female patients, whom they diagnosed as 'depressed', to their domestic role.

On the basis of such studies feminist sociologists contend that doctors act as agents of society and maintain the status quo as far as their female patients are concerned by adjusting them to their domestic roles. It is not suggested that they do this consciously, merely that this is the thrust of present prescribing patterns. In general, doctors aim to return patients to their pre-illness condition; they do not see it as their function to consider whether that condition brought about the illness in the first place, and may do so again.

STUDYING NEUROTICS: THE WOMEN AND MEN OF THE PRESENT RESEARCH

The research which forms the basis of this book was carried out with the help and co-operation of sixty-five women who gave generously of their time and talked at length to the researchers about their lives. In addition, twenty men agreed to participate in the study and the information they gave was contrasted with that gained from the women. All respondents were married and living with their spouses, and at the start of the study their ages ranged from 20 to 55. All had been referred to a psychiatrist for the first time and been diagnosed as suffering from a neurotic disorder; they had all started some kind of psychiatric treatment on an out-patient basis. The two interviewers (the author and a woman colleague) talked with each respondent soon after their first meeting with the psychiatrists in order to hear about their lives before the psychiatric referral and their views concerning the referral and diagnosis. These interview-talks were repeated a year later, to note the changes that might have taken place and to learn something about their psychiatric treatment from the viewpoint of the patients. Nearly half of the women (thirty) were asked to discuss changes in their lives for a third and last time a further year later.

Respondents were identified through the psychiatric services.

They were selected according to criteria established by the research design, i.e. they were married, living with their spouses, of working age, referred to a psychiatrist for the first time, diagnosed as neurotic and recommended for out-patient treatment. There was no other element of pre-selection, and the chosen individuals were taken consecutively from those who had been referred to psychiatrists in the research area after a given date. They were approached by letter, sent to them either through the psychiatrists or directly, with their agreement. The psychiatrists could prevent the inclusion of any of their patients, but they excluded only a few, all on the grounds that they were too upset to talk to a researcher. (For example, two women had just learned that their children suffered from serious diseases, and another that her child was mentally handicapped; three others were nursing terminally ill husbands).

Of the potential respondents who were approached, very few refused to take part in the study: the response rate was 85 per cent. Although it was carefully explained, in the introductory letter sent to potential respondents, that there was no pressure on them to take part, it eventually came to light that some felt reluctant to refuse to participate in a study approved by their psychiatrists. (The fact that the letters went via, or by permission of, the psychiatrists was taken to indicate their approval. Initial reluctance became apparent usually when an interview was over; several women said warmly how much they had enjoyed the talk and the chance to 'discuss things with an outsider', even though they had been apprehensive at first.

In recent years critics of the research enterprise have raised the question of the possible exploitation of respondents, i.e. that their time, enthusiasm attention and energy are being used in the interest of the researchers (Finch and Groves, 1983; Oakley, 1981A; Wilkinson, 1986). The usual justification of researchers is the hope that their findings will be of help to their respondents and others, and it was on this premise that help from respondents was sought in the present study. It was aimed to make the talks as pleasant, relaxed and informal as possible, without restriction of time, so that respondents could chatter on for as long as they wanted to. The researchers felt that to lend a willing ear was little enough return for taking up people's time.

Interviews took place in the homes and, in the event, lasted for a minimum of one, and a maximum of four, hours.

During the interviews the individuals participating in the study talked about their lives, experiences and feelings. In many traditional sociological and medical surveys, reports by individuals of their experiences and of the subjective meaning that they attach to them, are little valued, if not entirely discounted, in search of 'objective' information. The tendency to devalue 'self-reporting' is even stronger if the individuals under study happen to be women and stronger still if they are labelled mentally ill. Feminist sociologists point out that women's experiences, as perceived by themselves, are often disregarded by 'mainstream' social scientists and medical researchers, who are likely to be male and to write from a male perspective (Roberts, 1981A; Finch and Groves, 1983). When the subjects of the study are psychiatric patients, another problem arises: traditionally, health professionals have interpreted information from people whom they consider to be disturbed as distortion reflecting a sick mind (Goffman, 1961; Rosenhan, 1973). Thus, from a woman diagnosed as suffering from depression, her report that she receives little help from her family would be regarded as a reflection of her depressed state, not necessarily to be given credence. When there exists a strong stereotype, such as that of the 'neurotic woman' who always complains and magnifies her troubles, the temptation for both professionals and lay people is to disregard statements made by women labelled neurotic, especially if these statements take the form of complaints, thus confirming the stereotype. The intention in this research was to take information gained from the women, and the men, seriously, and to explore their assessments of their situation.

No assumption was made that all the respondents were suffering from neurosis, even though they had been so diagnosed. Questions of whether neurosis exist and, if so, what it is, and whether all those diagnosed really suffer from it, were regarded as problematic. The starting point was that being referred to a psychiatrist, diagnosed as suffering from a disorder and receiving psychiatric treatment, constitutes a social reality, one which was commonly experienced by all respondents in the research.

This study was based on a total of 200 interviews with sixty-five women and twenty men. In addition, information about these women and men was obtained from a register of psychiatric patients. In computerised form, details of diagnosis, treatment, contact with psychiatric services and social information (e.g. age, occupation, household composition etc.) were made available.

The main focus of the research was on the experiences of the female psychiatric patients who exceeded, by more than three times, the numbers of their male counterparts in the sample. This circumstance confirmed epidemiological findings of a marked gender difference in rates of neurosis, suggesting that neurotic disorder can be considered predominantly a female problem. Furthermore, as the interviews progressed it became evident that the women respondents were more ready to talk about themselves to the researchers. This could have been because women, in general, are more willing to discuss their personal lives than are men, or it may have been that the researchers, women themselves, could more easily establish rapport with those of their own sex. Certainly, in depth and in volume more information was forthcoming from the women than from the men, who tended to be taciturn.

Another reason for focussing mainly on the women was that there exists considerable evidence that the nature and causes of many social and emotional problems are different for men and, ideally, should be analysed separately. Even so, as said earlier, it was purposed to use the information gained from the men as a contrast, and in Chapters 2, 5 and 7, concerned respectively with making sense of neurosis, social support, and progress during the year, this proved to be possible. In Chapters 4 and 6, dealing respectively with stigma and encounters with professional helpers, the information gained from both sets of respondents was considered together. However, work, the subject of Chapter 3, had such different import for the men and women, and their respective work experiences were so unlike, that no meaningful comparison seemed possible; therefore, in Chapter 3 only women are considered.

The interviews with the women turned out to be less formal and more relaxed than those with the men, and to highlight this difference in the book female respondents are referred to by first names and male respondents by both first and second names. All names used are fictitious and every effort has been made to conceal the identity of the respondents.

2 Making Sense of Neurosis

THE IMPORTANCE OF THE LABEL

To receive a diagnosis of neurotic illness and be told that psychiatric treatment is the appropriate remedy, constitutes a shattering event in the life of an individual, and one with incalculable personal and social consequences.

Sociologists have emphasised the social significance of attaching to an individual a label, especially one that is negatively evaluated by society, e.g. 'alcoholic', 'shoplifter' and 'mad'. (The main features of the labelling perspective were discussed in Chapter 1). Studies of deviance first demonstrated the social consequences of negative labelling: the social standing, prestige and reputation of persons so labelled are adversely affected and their self-perception, behaviour and personal relationships are likely to undergo change (Becker, 1963). In a classic essay, Edwin Lemert developed the notion of 'secondary deviance', which he applied to situations in which people, on being labelled 'deviant', assume a new social role as deviants, which then takes over as their dominant role in society. Lemert distinguished this from 'primary deviance' i.e. the hidden, transitory or occasional aberrations of those who otherwise play ordinary social roles (Lemert, 1951).

Many social pressures incline the labelled person to acceptance of the label. Understanding and, where applicable, treatment, will follow upon acceptance: disapproval and sanctions will be the outcome of rejection. It has been demonstrated that deviant labels are frequently accepted by the labelled, who then increasingly conform to expectations and behave in accordance with their new role. Labelling becomes a self-fulfilling prophecy.

Labels, whether negatively or positively evaluated, imply social stereotypes. Blind people are stereotypically quiet, docile, well-behaved and cheerful in adversity and to that social image they are expected to conform (Scott, 1969). Once the label is accepted, self-perception and behaviour may well change (Higgins, 1980). The expectations and actions of the people around them constantly reaffirm labelled individuals in the social roles that have been assigned to them.

This process of self-fulfilling prophecy can be observed outside as well as within the field of deviance; for example, a child labelled 'intelligent' may perform better than another, of the same innate ability, labelled 'dull'. Illness, like deviance, is a social concept, and attaching the name 'illness' to a condition has social consequences (Freidson, 1970). Individuals, so labelled, may abandon, at least temporarily, their customary social activities, assume the sick role and thereafter conform to the social expectations attaching thereto. When a heart condition, multiple sclerosis or some other life-threatening or disabling disease is diagnosed, self-perception and behaviour may change markedly as the individual concerned adjusts his or her thinking and life-style to that popularly thought appropriate to the disease in question, to an extent possibly unwarranted by the disease process itself. Such changes, and the ensuing reassessment of relationships with others, are consequential to the received label (Miles, 1979; Knudson-Cooper, 1981).

Mental illness is a field in which labelling can have quite devastating consequences. It carries a peculiarly powerful and lasting cultural stereotype, resistant to change and extremely negatively evaluated.

If knowledge of the diagnosis is attended by such adverse effects, it may be asked whether doctors should rather not tell. They may be unaware of the social processes that they set in motion, as is quite likely with regard to physical illness. However, the potentially harmful effect of labelling someone mentally ill is well known to many physicians, who nevertheless feel that revealing the diagnosis is essential if suitable treatment is to be initiated. Moreover, studies of doctor-patient relationships demonstrate that the most frequent criticism of doctors by patients is that they receive inadequate information (Cartwright and Anderson, 1981; Stimson and Webb, 1975).

People want to know, even if the diagnosis is of a feared disease with poor prognosis, because they need to take decisions and make plans in the light of adequate information (Cartwright, 1970; Miles, 1979). They feel that they have a right to know what is happening to their own bodies.

There is another reason for this desire to know the diagnosis. Michael Balint, a physician with immense experience of general practice, pointed out that 'nearly always this is the chief and most immediate problem: the request for a name for the illness' (1964, p. 25). Balint argued that a patient who is not given the diagnosis may be alarmed.

Apart from the almost universal fear that what we have found is so frightening that we will not tell him, he feels that 'nothing wrong' means only that we have not found out and therefore cannot tell him what it is that frightens or worries him and causes him pain. Thus he feels let down, unable to explain and accept his pain, fears and deprivation.

Giving it a name implies, to the patient, that the condition is understood, known to medical science, and is treatable.

Thus, for a variety of reasons, people seek, and usually receive, a name for whatever condition is troubling them.

All of the respondents in the present study had been referred to psychiatrists, mostly by their doctors, and had started some form of psychiatric treatment. Whatever diagnostic name they were given, or themselves used, referral to a psychiatrist meant to them that they had a condition for which psychiatric treatment was considered appropriate by those assumed to possess knowledge of the subject.

In the light of their newly-acquired label 'psychiatric patients' these people attempted to assess what had happened to them and tried to make sense of their experiences. Very commonly, people in such situations ask themselves: how did it happen? How did I get into this state? Trying to find answers can involve an often agonising reappraisal of one's life; a rethinking of the conduct, relationships and events of one's pre-illness existence and a reassessment of one's self-image.

In this chapter the women's, and to a lesser extent the men's search for meanings and explanations will be explored. First, though, it may be of interest to consider the diagnostic categories to which the patients were assigned by the psychiatrists and the lay expressions used by the patients themselves to describe the disorders which had brought them into treatment.

DESCRIPTION OF THE PROBLEM

Diagnosis gives a name to a patient's ailment. Making a diagnosis can be described as a 'process of synthesising key features of a case into a clinical picture' (Mishler, 1981, p. 145); and by some it is seen as an art rather than a scientific procedure (Blaxter, 1978). Many diagnostic categories are surrounded by uncertainties, and psychiatric practice—perhaps more than any other medical speciality—has had the reliability of its diagnoses questioned. Nevertheless, a patient entering psychiatric treatment is assigned to a diagnostic category, if for no other reason, in the interest of record keeping. This diagnosis may or may not be communicated to the patient; and when it is, medical terminology may frequently be substituted by popular descriptions which are presumed by clinicians to be more easily understood by their patients.

Table 2.1A: Diagnosis by psychiatrists

Diagnostic categories	Women n = 65	Men n = 20
Neurotic depression	30	8
Anxiety states	17	5
Phobic states	16	4
Obsessive/compulsive disorders	2	—
Sexual problems	—	3

Table 2.1B: Description of problems by women and men

Descriptions*	Women n = 65	Men n = 20
Nervous problems/conditions	36	6
Depression	23	3
Nervous breakdown	20	—
Anxious type	14	—
Agoraphobia	10	—
Other phobias (e.g. spiders, germs, cats).	6	—
Nervous exhaustion	—	8
Drinking problems	—	7
Impotence	—	2

*More than one expression was used by respondents to describe their problems.

Their medical records showed that the sixty-five women of the study had all been assigned, by the psychiatrists treating them, to the general category of 'neuroses', sub-classified as thirty suffering from 'neurotic depression', seventeen from 'anxiety states', sixteen from 'phobic states' (including agoraphobia (ten), claustrophobia and animal phobias) and two from 'obsessive-compulsive disorders'.

The twenty men similarly assigned to the 'neuroses' category comprised eight suffering from 'neurotic depression', five from 'anxiety states', four from 'phobic states', and three from 'sexual problems'.

What psychiatrists tell their patients concerning diagnosis, prognosis and treatment and what their patients understand them to say, will be discussed elsewhere. It is sufficient to note here that, especially in early communications, psychiatrists (as indeed physicians in general) are reluctant to mention formal medical categorisations. Rather they talk vaguely of a 'little depression' or a 'nervous state'. But, whatever the words used, vague or precise, minimising the problem or spelling it out, the nature of the illness is inherent in the psychiatric referral itself: the label 'psychiatric patient' applies.

Health professionals and lay people describe illness in a variety of ways, formal and informal, clinical and colloquial.

Doctors and patients by no means always employ the same word for the same condition; indeed the women and men studied here used only two terms corresponding to formal psychiatric categories: depression and agoraphobia. The former has become common currency, more acceptable and seemingly less esoteric than other psychiatric usages; 'agoraphobia' was the term employed by women members of the relevant self-help groups. Not surprisingly, more than a third of the women described their problems as 'depression' while other frequently-mentioned appellatives, in descending order, were: nervous problem/condition, breakdown, anxiety, agoraphobia and panic. There were also a few references to obsessions and to nervous tension. Quite a number of the women, in an endearingly personalised way, would say 'my depression', or 'my breakdown' (perhaps echoing the colloquial 'my period'). No one referred to 'illness' or 'sickness' during the interviews; it was always 'my problem started . . .' or 'I've had these troubles since I was a teenager' (see Table 2.2)

Table 2.2: Most frequently mentioned symptoms of neurosis

	Women n = 65	Men n = 20
Emotional symptoms:		
Feeling low or depressed	41	4
Constant feelings of worry and anxiety	25	—
Irritable, quarrelsome	20	—
Specific fears (of dirt, animals, going out, etc.)	14	—
Panic attacks	11	4
Drinking too much	8	7
Physical symptoms:		
Sleeplessness	22	—
Breathlessness	16	10
Sweating	15	6
Weight loss	9	—
Weight gain	7	—
Gone off sex	—	5

The word 'symptoms' did not come up during discussions of how problems manifested themselves, nevertheless a wide range of complaints came to light, both emotional and physical. The most often mentioned were: feelings of worry and anxiety, irritability, shouting at children, having rows, feeling low (terrible, poorly), attacks of panic, and wanting to stay in bed and not do anything. Less frequently, mention was made of specific problems, such as drinking too much, inability to eat, fear of spiders, etc.

Researchers often try to categorise the problems presented to psychiatrists as 'emotional', 'physical', or 'social' (Kadushin, 1969). Interestingly, the complaints voiced by the respondents in this study were multifarious and did not easily lend themselves to this sort of categorisation. Rather, they were presented as a combination of many kinds of difficulties which, in the aggregate, produced a general malaise, a feeling that something was wrong. This was especially true of the women whose troubles could almost be summed up in one phrase, 'I can't cope'.

Sandra, 31, two children 5 and 12: 'I am terribly afraid that I am going to die . . . I know I am hypochondriac and it worries me terribly . . . I shout at the children, I feel so irritable with them, I know it's wrong . . . I am worried about my heart, I feel breathless and my heart is bumping, but the tests show it's alright . . . I am so poorly on some days, I feel I can't cope'.

Susan, 21, no children: 'I feel depressed and worried . . . some days I feel I can't go on and I shut myself away . . . I have dreadful rows with my husband; after one row I tried to cut my wrists, just in anger you know, it wasn't serious . . . I cry a lot and feel terrible . . . I think I have agoraphobia a bit, I don't want to go out . . . I can't cope very well, I feel too irritable'.

Typically, complaints were diffuse as is very often the case with the presentation of symptoms, both physical and psychological. Studies have shown that a lack of coherence and specificity is characteristic of the way people describe their health problems (Balint, 1957; Byrne and Long, 1976; Mishler, 1981). The unfocussed way in which clusters of problems were described to the interviewers showed that a single specific disease entity was far from the thinking of these women, even when a diagnosis of 'neurosis' was communicated to them.

The men's complaints were less diffuse, and of a different nature: they described their problems largely without reference to emotional states. Only three used the term 'depression', the others reported nervous exhaustion, (or just 'exhaustion'), drinking problems and 'attacks'. In more detailed accounts of how their problems manifested themselves, they spoke of taking an overdose, going off sex, having heart and other physical troubles, or 'going berserk'.

In general, the ways in which people describe their health and well-being, at any particular time, are the product of complex social processes in which prevailing health norms, expectations concerning acceptable levels of well-being, interpretations of particular features of life as problematic, interaction with doctors and a variety of other factors all play a part. In a number of studies the processes which result in people presenting themselves in doctors' consulting rooms have been demonstrated. (Robinson, 1971; Stimson and Webb, 1975; Miles, 1987).

THE SEARCH FOR CAUSES

Both women and men struggled to understand and make sense of their situations as psychiatric patients, but they differed in the kinds of explanation they considered and the extent of their search for solutions. The women appeared to have thought much more about possible causes of their problems and their various explanations will now be discussed, with a brief description of the men's thoughts on the subject. It is not suggested that the women took their predicament as psychiatric patients more seriously: men appeared much affected by this label also. But the women, much more so than the men, discarded easy and superficial explanations and searched for personally satisfactory answers.

To present the individual explanations of respondents under

specific headings (relationships with husband, the family, hardships in life etc.), is to distort reality in the interest of analytical order. Social scientists commonly face this difficulty; in their attempt to bring some order into a bewildering complex accumulation of feelings, speculations, truths and half-truths gained from their informants, they have to break down the subject matter into manageable parts. In so doing, they distort the social world they seek to represent. As one investigator remarked, the researcher is taunted by the 'paradox of ordinary reality versus the unreality of order' (Davis, 1963, p. 19).

The categorisation of the disease explanations put forward by the men and women attempted in the following pages is not intended to suggest that the respondents, generally, considered possible explanations in a systematic, orderly, sequential way. On the contrary, their efforts for the most part were characterised by confusion, vacillation and ambiguity, as they considered, discarded and considered again, explanations that occurred or had been suggested to them. They often described their attempts to understand what happened in their lives in terms such as 'I have thought and thought and I get confused but I have to go on'; 'It took me a long time to puzzle it out'; 'The more I think the more confusing it all becomes'.

Table 2.3: Most frequently considered causes of neurosis

	Women n = 65	Men n = 20
Unsatisfactory marriage	32	—
Past actions	25	—
Hormone-changes: PMT, menopause, post-natal	25	—
Unsatisfactory family relationships	18	—
Caring for sick, disabled or elderly relative	13	—
Adverse life-events	11	4
Childhood experiences	8	1
Problems at work	3	11
Physical illness or surgery	3	10

Past actions as explanations

Most people, on learning that they are suffering from a medical condition, will want to know the cause of it, in a medical/biological sense. Was it a virus? Is it hereditary? etc., are questions likely to be directed to the doctor who may or may not provide a satisfactory answer. But in cases of a serious, long-term, physical or mental illness there is another question directed elsewhere: 'Why me?' By this, some personal responsibility is imputed—'What have I done to deserve this/Why have I been singled out in this way?'

Even when an illness is such that the person hit by it would not be thought by prevailing social expectations to have been negligent, or otherwise responsible for the condition, the search for an explanation in terms of past conduct may still be pursued. Thus, after a heart attack people ask themselves whether they could have avoided it by working more calmly, striving less for promotion, avoiding quarrels and over-excitement. In a study concerned with children who contracted polio, (at a time when vaccine was not available), a father blamed himself for his son's paralysis, arguing that it would not have happened had he not decided to move in search of better prospects (Davis, 1963).

Explanations in terms of one's own actions are attractive because they accord with the wish to be in control of one's life. The feeling that the environment, one's small world, can be controlled is important (Parsons, 1958); if one's actions caused or contributed to illness or other problems, these are likely to be amenable to improvement by further and different actions. On the other hand a sense of helplessness in the face of a hostile uncontrollable environment detracts from life's meaning and makes one's actions seem futile.

As Table 2.3 indicates, past actions were considered by twenty-five of the women, as they sought to explain their neurosis:

Fiona, 29, three children 3, 9 and 11: 'One day I brought an injured bird home and the day after that Timmy got sick (youngest child, 3½) I blamed myself for bringing the disease into the house. The doctor said Timmy's infection had nothing to do with the bird but I've blamed myself for it ever since. When someone is sick, I think I must have brought disease into the house again' (Fiona described her problem as 'germ phobia' and 'being obsessive about filth').

No fewer than eighteen women cited actions connected with the reproductive process: to have or not to have a child, pregnancy and abortion.

Molly, 23, two children 2 and 6: 'I was pregnant when I was sixteen, my boy-friend was 18, his parents made him say he'd have nothing to do with me. My parents wanted me to have an abortion, but I said no, I am going to have the baby. When Nicky was born, I was ill, then depressed, I wasn't really ready to have a child then. I ran away for nearly two years, left the baby with my mother, it was terrible for her. I think when I decided to have the baby, and not to have an abortion, I started all my nervous troubles. I love Nicky now and try to make up for it, but still, I caused my own troubles'. (Nicola, 6 years old, thought to be dyslexic).

Fiona and Molly both attributed their problems to specific happenings for which they felt guilty. Others, too, reassessed past actions in the light of the diagnostic label, mentioning such matters as a failure to nurse a sick relative, not giving up work when a child was born, leaving home as a teenager, discontinuing education, and marrying young or for the wrong reason.

This process of exploration rarely provided the women with answers which did more than partly account for their subsequent difficulties but it enhanced their feelings of guilt and responsibility.

Relationships with husbands
A significant message reaching the woman entering into psychiatric treatment for neurosis is that she should look to her relationships with her family when seeking the causes of her problems. She is quite likely to be told this in the consulting room; in any case psychiatrists, psychologists etc, make this point to the general public via the media. In a popular book, Dorothy Rowe (1983), a clinical psychologist, writing sympathetically on the subject of depression, tells how she

usually points out to her patients 'that depression is not something inside a person, it is the way that person relates to himself and the people around him' (p. 147). At their first meeting, the psychiatrist will routinely record the patient's life history and ask questions concerning relationships with close relatives. For a married woman, this will involve a discussion of her life with her husband and serve to focus her attention on a possible connection between their marital relations and her neurotic illness.

Almost half of the women attributed their troubles, at least partially, to an unhappy marriage but for the most part they looked for other causes also, feeling that their problems were too complex to admit of a facile solution. In describing their marital difficulties the question of blame loomed large. Kim and Marjorie blamed their husbands:

Kim, 28, three daughters 3, 7 and 9: 'He was always violent, from the beginning . . . just after we were married, he beat me so badly that I left him. I was only seventeen and a half, but I didn't really have anywhere else to go, so I went back to him . . . he didn't change, the last time he beat me was when Sal was ill (youngest child, chest infection) and I told him that I couldn't stand another night with no sleep'.

Marjory, 41, three sons 15, 18 and 23: 'I think the root of Mick's trouble is his drinking because he is alright when he doesn't touch it. When he drinks he is terrible at night, he come home late, wakes me up sometimes five or six times for sex, then just falls asleep. The last time he got drunk in the evening he came home in a terrible state, shouting at us and broke the banister, then smashed the window. We didn't want the police but the neighbour called them. They put him in a cell for the night. Next day I was driving to my sister when I had a terrible panic attack, I usually have a bad one after trouble with Mick, it shows that's the root of my trouble'.

Other women felt that they, as well as their husbands, were responsible for the home situation. Typically, they said that although their husbands were inconsiderate, violent or in some other way unsatisfactory, they themselves, by being too meek or submissive, by offering provocation or just by not leaving him, were also to blame.

Bridget, 29, two children 4 and 7: 'He is violent sometimes, but not very often . . . the trouble is more that he doesn't show any affection, doesn't really care about the children. . . he shouts at us, well, really it's me most of the time, not so much the children . . . he uses terrible language when he is angry. He says to me, when we make up, you know, that it makes him angry to see me cringe and afraid . . . I know I should shout back and stand up for myself, but I can't. I just feel frozen inside. It's not my fault, but it's not his either, really, he can't help being what he is, he was born that way . . . his mother says he got it from his Dad. The trouble is, it affects my nerves and I get nightmares . . . I know my nervous problem is caused by this'.

Kay, 35, no children: 'I tried many times to get him to go for treatment, but he always refused [husband is a chronic alcoholic]. I know I have only myself to blame, I should have left him when he refused, but I can't do it. My family thinks I should leave him, even the doctor said it may give him a shock and then he would accept the treatment. I can't bring myself to it, not because I love him, nobody can love him the way he is now. So, I ended up by having treatment for my nerves, instead of him'.

Studies concerned with violence against women show that women tend to accept responsibility for such crimes. For example, women who are raped may share the view that the victim probably provoked the attack (Hanmer and Saunders, 1983). Similarly, in this study, women with violent and aggressive husbands had a tendency to shoulder some of the blame themselves on the basis that they must, somehow, have provoked the husband's behaviour. Marion and Liz blamed themselves for their unsatisfactory marriages:

Marion, 33, three children 9, 10 and 13: 'I neglected Paul [husband], I always loved the children more, all my love has gone to them. . . I am very close to my twin, this is something people can't understand, I mean if you haven't got a twin you don't understand. I was closer to Barbara than to Paul and he was jealous. He is right, I know that, it's my fault entirely, but the truth is, well, it is hard to say this, but while I have my children and Barbara is near me, I don't really need Paul. I know I should not feel like this'. (Marion and Barbara are identical twins, Barbara is divorced from her husband and has one child).

Liz, 29, no children, referring to an unsatisfactory sexual relationship with her husband said 'it was never very good, I never felt keen or interested but I wanted a child so much. Now that I know I can't have one, I don't want sex either'.

In a minority of cases neither party was held responsible for the unhappy marriage:

Cheryl, 29, two children 4 and 6, also mentioned an unsatisfactory sex life, saying that there was a natural loss of interest after eleven years of marriage which was not the fault of either of them. 'Sex became routine, I don't enjoy it, I just go through with it'.

Lisa, three children 3, 7 and 9: 'We just drifted apart. We have nothing in common, we don't like the same things. He is a loner, doesn't like company, when he is upset he goes for a long drive by himself. I like to be with people, like the children to bring their friends . . . I like to go out with them, Kenneth doesn't come. He likes his books and music, he is very serious . . . I don't like his kind of TV programmes. We are not compatible and it's a very unhappy state of affairs, but neither of us can help it . . . it is very difficult to live like this in the same house, but it's for the sake of the children. I think sometimes it would be better if we separated . . . I wonder if it would be worse for the children'?

The search for explanations, the effort to bring meaning to a situation fraught with uncertainty was made more difficult for those women who assumed that some factor out of the ordinary was needed to account for their neurosis. People, generally, will accept as normal all manner of aches and pains, and the ups and downs of life, sudden or developing slowly over a long time, provided these are prevalent with their own social group. So to pinpoint the unsatisfactory elements of a deteriorating marriage was not, for these women, sufficient to explain their neurosis, there had to be some other, extraordinary, explanation. Certainly, Kim, and Marjorie, Bridget and Kay, located their troubles in their exceptionally unhappy domestic situations but others, like Lisa, denied that a bad marriage could be the main cause because many people in like case coped nevertheless.

> *Lisa* (again) 'I know my marriage is not unique, there are many like us, who are incompatible. I look at my cousin who is married to an Irishman, they don't have anything in common, either, but they get along somehow. Why is it that I can't cope better? Perhaps none of this had anything to do with my breakdown after all'.

So Lisa, who first cited an unhappy marriage as the cause of her neurosis, came to think, on reflection, that maybe the real reason lay elsewhere. She was not alone in this.

Family troubles

Relationships with parents, children, siblings and in-laws were all examined by the women in their search to explain neurosis. No doubt, for many people, strained relationships and disagreements with relatives are part of daily life and there is usually some difficulty which can be picked up and examined in the light of a new development, such as the beginning of psychiatric treatment. Nevertheless, most of the women discarded family troubles as sole causes, although these 'didn't help'. Those who did ascribe their nervous problems to causes of this kind seemed to have experienced exceptionally severe difficulties, often culminating in a crisis. For example, Ann's two children from a former marriage had an ongoing bad relationship with their stepfather and failed to get on with their half-brother (the child of the current marriage); they blamed their mother. The situation erupted with two simultaneous pregnancies.

Ann, 41, three children 8, 16 and 18: 'At the end of last year I was pregnant again. I knew it would bring more trouble at home, I didn't know what to do . . . then came the shock, my daughter Cindy suddenly told us that she, too, was pregnant. She hadn't wanted to tell us, wanted to go away and come back with the baby, she said, but her boyfriend's parents put pressure on her to have an abortion. She wanted me to go and talk to them, so I went and Ben [husband] came too and we landed up having a row. Of course, it didn't help with Cindy and I both at home, and my nerves gave way. I couldn't stand the whole thing any more'.

The two pregnancies, coming on top of an already badly strained family situation, constituted a burden which Ann held to be the cause of her nervous troubles. (Unhappily, both pregnancies ended tragically: Ann had a miscarriage followed by sterilisation, Cindy's premature baby died).

Margaret was another who blamed her condition on a complex domestic situation.

Margaret, 42, three daughters 11,13 and 16: 'I tried to puzzle it out for a long time; what caused it all? Why did I get this depression? I got very depressed after the attack on Jackie (youngest daughter, aged 10, sexually attacked by a man of 83) it brought back to me the time when I was first pregnant. It was quite different, but it all came back. (Margaret's first daughter was conceived when she was 15½ at a holiday camp, father unknown.) Then Jackie was questioned by the police and had a lot of attention for months and started to behave as if everybody owed her something. She liked being the centre of attention. The other two became jealous and started to play up. I got more and more depressed and the last straw was when my mother told Molly (eldest daughter) that she had a stepfather, not a real father. I thought about it a lot, did my mother want to make trouble or did it just slip out? I can't help blaming my mother because now everybody is upset and things go from bad to worse'.

For Ann and Margaret, their neurosis was rooted in their family troubles. But the majority of the women whose troubles could be so categorised went on looking for the elusive 'something else' that would provide them with a more satisfactory solution. Thus,

> *June, 35, four children 2, 8, 13 and 16:* 'I felt very depressed when my family cut me off. It was after my brother James behaved so badly to his wife, he always drank too much, and one day he was drunk, broke all the furniture with a hammer and even smashed the windscreen of his car . . . I supported my sister-in-law, she is nice and had suffered enough. My whole family treated me as a traitor, my mother and my other brother said I should have supported my own flesh and blood . . . . My mother started to tell tales about me to my husband . . . they hardly ever speak to me now and I feel terrible . . . . But these things happen in families and I shouldn't be depressed like this . . . . There must be something else'.

Severe difficulties and adverse events

Some of the women sought explanations in a combination of circumstances which made their lives exceptionally difficult and which they regarded as being beyond their, or anyone's, control and amenable neither to change nor solution.

Perhaps the most severe difficulties were those reported by the thirteen women who had, for a long time, looked after chronic sick or disabled members of their families.

> *Pat, 29, two children 2 and 6:* 'I knew something was wrong with Glen very soon . . . when they told me what was wrong I didn't understand [younger child Glen has cystic fibrosis]. They explained it to me in the hospital, and they told me what to do, but they didn't tell me what it was going to do to my life'.

> *Peggy, 40, four children, daughter 13, son 15, twins 18:* 'I always had a struggle with the twins, never a time without problems [twins are spastic and mentally handicapped] . . . daily grind, morning to night work and worry . . . I tried to make up for it to the other two, so that they didn't lose out much, but I couldn't even do that. My youngest had to help

out when the twins were growing up and became more difficult. I am not surprised that she couldn't stand it' (13-year-old daughter ran away from home, brought back by police).

Kate, 21, one baby son: 'When I was seventeen my father had lung cancer. The doctors said he was terminally ill and had six months to live. I lived in the house, alone with him, for 18 months, then he died. I never left the house in those months, didn't go out once, the neighbour did our shopping and the doctor called. After my father died I found I couldn't go out. I panicked at the thought of leaving the house. It was only later that I knew it was agoraphobia'.

Peggy, Pat and Kate had sole responsibility for nursing and looking after the distressed members of their families, So had May, 54 years old, whose husband became partially paralysed after a stroke, Jenny, 34, whose mother was schizophrenic, and others, variously looking after senile parents and disabled relatives.

Much evidence has been accumulated about the home-nursing role of women (Graham, 1984). Sick children are nursed by their mothers, disabled and mentally ill relatives are looked after by the women of the family, and geriatric parents are nursed by daughters and daughters-in-law. In general, provision of long-term home care for the sick and handicapped is provided, in contemporary society, by women and this continues to be the case even for women who have paid employment outside the home. It is also evidenced that these female carers tend to neglect their own health; studies on the impact of living with a mentally ill relative have demonstrated the ill-effects on the carer's physical and psychological well-being (Grad and Sainsbury, 1968). Several women in the study spoke about their daily routine of housework and home nursing: a relentless, early morning to late evening round of work, often supplemented by demands and recriminations from their fretful charges. Research on housework (Oakley, 1974), found that housewives work an average of 77 hours per week; this was the workload of women who did not also have chronically sick or handicapped relatives to look after! The women carers of the present study described being constantly tired through lack of sleep and being forever on call. Perhaps, even worse were other features of their situation, the hopelessness of finding a way out and guilt-feeling that in spite of all the work they put in their efforts were inadequate. This feeling of inadequacy was experienced by several women: Peggy thought that she had let down her 13-year-old daughter, by not protecting her from disagreeable sights attendant upon the task of looking after the spastic retarded twins; other felt, similarly, that their healthy children suffered by the diversion of attention from them to the handicapped. Several suggested that the caring task itself was too onerous to be done really well.

Not all of the thirteen women carers had spent a life-time in that role. Those who had, regarded it as sufficient explanation of their neurotic condition. Typically, they commented 'it's enough to give depression to anyone' and 'no wonder I ended up like this'.

Other women attempted to understand their problems in terms of what sociologists call 'adverse life events', although only two of them, a social worker and a nurse, used this term.

Wendy, 26, two children 5 and 6: 'I got depressed after my baby died, I couldn't get over it [third child, born prematurely, died in incubator due to underdeveloped lungs] . . . I couldn't accept what happened. One day I ran down the street, shouting it was not my baby who died . . . I was treated for depression then . . . I was better when I was pregnant again and then came a miscarriage. I became really depressed . . . I couldn't get out of my head that I must be a bad mother to my children and I don't deserve another baby . . .'

A few women talked of bereavements and other losses culminating in nervous breakdowns.

Liz (again): 'The first blow was when I found out that I can never have a child. I always wanted children and I built my life around it. I dropped out of dental school when I married because my husband was posted abroad, and we counted on children coming along. When I finally had to come to terms with not having children I had to review my whole life, my marriage, everything . . .. My husband gave me a pet dog to keep me company and I became very fond of her. For years she was a constant companion, so intelligent that I could talk to her . . . then I lost her and I felt terrible, I can't explain it . . . on top of that came the news that my sister-in-law had a terminal illness. I had a breakdown'.

Life events are notoriously difficult to assess in terms of their emotional meaning for the individual concerned. Reaction to the loss of a much loved pet may be more profound in its emotional content that appears to an outside observer; Liz couldn't bear to talk about the disease and death of her dog and cried whenever she was reminded of it. Her dying sister-in-law was also her closest friend, the person she named as her main confidante and support. The coming together of these life events provided, for her, an adequate explanation of her breakdown;

For some, an adverse event provided not a complete explanation of the problem, but rather a trigger, a 'last straw' in a whole difficult situation. For example, Bridget said that she coped well enough with her violent husband while she had the constant help and support of her 'Nan'. But then her 'Nan' died and Bridget's breakdown followed.

Interestingly, women who considered that the hardships of their daily lives provided a full or partial explanation of their neurotic problems, tended to take into account only the most severe circumstances and events which they regarded as being outside the range of ordinary problems which were accepted as 'women's lot'.

Physical causes

Many psychiatric patients choose to attribute their condition to physical causes. Physical illness is socially more acceptable, less stigmatised and less feared than mental illness. It is also easier and pleasanter to account for problems in biophysical terms than to examine well-established relationships and to assess critically one's past actions. These advantages, however, can sometimes lead people to think that physical illness or biophysical processes are 'easy options' as explanations, and thus should be discarded and replaced by a search for harder and more painful solutions, which, exactly because they are less easy, appear to be more valid.

Many women in the study sought explanations in physical causes but few felt entirely satisfied with such solutions when they found them. Hardly anyone attributed neurotic problems to physical illness but many tried to make sense of those problems in terms of natural female biological processes. Pre-mentrual tension, post-natal depression and the menopause were frequently discussed.

Menstruation and the menopause, linked with hormone changes, have often been held responsible for variations in the moods and behaviour of women. Stressing the importance of the 'Curse' and the 'Change' has been a double-edged argument. On the one hand, women often find it difficult to convince men (male doctors included) of the reality of the attendant physical discomfort or pain, menstrual and menopausal problems frequently being described by men as 'psychological', i.e. imaginary, states (Weidegar, 1978). On the other hand, women's biological processes have been cited throughout history to exclude them from high-status, responsible and powerful positions, as men have argued that their periodic instability renders women unsuitable for such positions (Parlee, 1976).

Women in the study found that it was often difficult to make the men around them understand their physical discomforts; when they succeeded the women found it equally difficult to avoid their natural processes being 'blown up' by their menfolk into all-important features of their nervous problems.

Pre-menstrual tension was the least mentioned of the three hormone-linked states, indeed, the idea of PMT as a problem is relatively new to many women; until recently it has received less publicity and been less widely discussed than the other two states. A few women mentioned PMT as contributing to their 'mood changes' or inability to cope but only two attributed their problems mainly to this cause.

Elsie, 38, three sons 10, 13 and 16: 'I am convinced that all my so-called depression is due to menstrual tension. I watched it very carefully and there is a monthly cycle, there is no way I could mistake that. For 10 days before menstruation I am at my worst, I am so irritable, I shout at everyone, no one can touch me. Sometimes I feel like murdering somebody, the tension is so great. When the menstruation starts it always gets better, immediate relief comes. But I am not really well between the periods either and you can't wonder, I know the next bad time is on the way, I know how I will feel the week after and I worry in advance. Unfortunately, they are all men in the family, they can't understand, I don't blame them but it doesn't help. I wish I had a sister or a mother'.

Elsie was rather defensive in her explanation because, she said, neither her family doctor, not her psychiatrist (both male) believed her. Nevertheless, she was one of the minority who did not search further for causes but felt she had achieved a satisfactory explanation.

Post-natal depression was more widely referred to, several women saying that they experienced it, although they didn't know what it was at the time. With hindsight, they thought it was the root of their problem. Others had been attended by health visitors, who explained the nature of post-natal depression and encouraged them to attribute their problems to this cause.

Christine, 30 two children 17 months and 3 years; currently pregnant: 'I had post-natal depression after each baby . . . I had it for months, both times . . . after Danny was born I felt terrible, weepy and low all the time, I couldn't cope at all, but I didn't know what it was, nobody told me . . . I felt so guilty, I thought I was a bad mother. After Frances was born I felt the same again but I had a marvellous Health Visitor and she told me it was post-natal depression . . . I still felt low and anxious, but somehow less worried, it is difficult to explain, but a little bit of the curtain lifted when the Health Visitor explained it. This time I am prepared, I know what to do when it comes'.

The menopause, as an explanation of problems, presented a similar picture: a few women accepted it as a satisfactory and complete explanation, rather more regarded it as contributing to their difficulties which were, however, likely to have been caused by other things. This latter view was exemplified by Ida, who mentioned the menopause as one item in an unhappy life.

Ida, 52, one son 25: 'My problem developed over a period of time. Neil [husband] and I are not suited to each other; it has never been a happy home . . . . He likes to regiment everything, the home must be run according to rules. I was hit by everything at the same time, the Change started and Stuart [son] went abroad. I couldn't adjust to things. I had a lot of problems with the Change, I know it is all hormonal, but it came at a bad time for me. Now I haven't got anything. It is not as if I could get work at my age. After Stuart left, we moved into this smaller place (three-bedroomed cottage); there is not much to do here. I am unlucky with the neighbours too, they are very noisy, you can hear them now'.

Childhood experiences

It became apparent to the interviewers that many of the women had picked up some knowledge of the significance accorded by psychiatrists to childhood experiences. People are exposed to the popularisation of medical matters via the media; there exists, also, the age-old informal exchange of information within social circles. It has to be added, that history-taking by psychiatrists can itself open up new areas of thinking by their patients.

The level of understanding of the women in this study ranged from the informed to the ignorant; from that of a social worker, a graduate in social anthropology and a psychiatric nurse, to that of those who knew little or nothing of psychiatric matters before they themselves were given a psychiatric diagnosis.

Never put forward as a sole cause, childhood experiences were cited by eight out of the sixty-five women as contributing to their neurosis. Emma was one example:

Emma, 36, three children 9, 13 and 16: 'It began a long time ago. Your childhood has a lot to do with it. My parents were very strict, I am sure they loved me, but couldn't show it. I was jealous of my younger brother, I knew my parents wanted a son to continue the family business and my brother was very important to them. I felt second-class compared to my brother. I had a breakdown when I was preparing for A levels, I tried to do too much, to show that I was as good as my brother . . . then too, I married the wrong personality, my husband makes me feel guilty when I have a guilt complex anyway. He says I don't love Timothy [son] as much as the girls, he says that I project my own feelings [concerning brother] on Timothy. He may be right. I know he thinks I am not a good housewife, he likes a strictly run home, everything on time, and he thinks I am not good at that . . . I also had a bit of a post-natal depression after the first two births, the third was much better . . . I think my trouble is being at home, I would be better for an outside job, but Cara is still very young, wouldn't know what to do in the holidays . . . I was very depressed when my Grandmother died, she was a mother to me when I needed her, always . . . this breakdown started when I thought I was pregnant and I didn't want another child. When I found that it was a mistake, I insisted on sterilisation, but it upset me too much'.

It might seem, to an outside observer, that Emma's troubles did indeed stem from her childhood experiences, but she didn't see it that way. For her, these had no greater significance than the other misfortunes mentioned in her rather rambling narrative.

FOCUS OF WOMEN: THE DOMESTIC SCENE

Thus, the women tried hard to explain to themselves why and how their neurotic problems developed and how they came to acquire the label 'psychiatric patient'. They concentrated on certain aspects of their lives, namely past actions, relationships within their immediate families, exceptional hardships, female biological processes and childhood experiences. A minority thereby arrived at a solution which seemed satisfactorily to explain their problems, but for the majority the cause they found constituted only a partial explanation and the struggle to make sense of their experiences continued.

In these efforts they concentrated almost exclusively on matters domestic. This is not surprising, as home and family loom large in women's lives. Numerous studies have shown that the socialisation of girls for the feminine gender role is bound up with the role of housewife and mother. For adult women, femininity itself tends to be equated with domesticity, and their self-image is integrated with their domestic role (Oakley, 1981B; Sharpe, 1984). Understandably, a woman trying to interpret an event as traumatic as becoming a psychiatric patient, is inclined to explore her domestic life as being of crucial importance. Moreover, psychiatrists and physicians tend to steer women patients towards a concentration on the family setting, thus reinforcing their self-perception as primarily wives and mothers (Cooperstock and Parnell, 1982).

In recent years sociologists have explored the division between the public domain of the workplace, politics and the state and the private domain of the family and domestic life (Garmanikov *et al.,* 1983A). The public domain consists of institutions and activities which have been, traditionally, male concerns (indeed, the bulk of women have been excluded from them) while the private domain has been regarded as mainly the concern of women. In this study women placed themselves and the roots of their neurotic problems firmly in the private sphere and did not look beyond its confines.

It is interesting to note that even those women who had outside employment concentrated on the private domain. Nearly half of the women in the study had full or part-time employment (thirty out of sixty-five) but their focus was in no way different from that of the full-time housewives. Neither did the women connect their problems to wider social issues; no one in their social circle or amongst their professional helpers suggested that they look at social structures as having a bearing on their problems. Thus no one questioned why nursing the sick and caring for the handicapped should fall on women in society; lack of suitable provision was not mentioned, let alone linked to the politics of providing services which would help women. Instead there was a general acceptance of the status quo, and the problem for women was seen as their inability to cope within the given structure.

THE MEN—BY CONTRAST

The twenty men of this study also tried to find explanations for their having become psychiatric patients but the possibilities they considered, and found acceptable, were different. Unlike the women, they appeared not to examine in any depth their marital relationships, nor their relationships with relatives. Either the message that neurosis is connected with personal relationships is less forcibly projected towards men, or men are less ready to allow it. It is, of course, possible that the media and psychiatric practice alike focus on women as the likely consumers of news about, and therapy for, neurosis. It may also be that women are the more inclined to look for explanations in terms of their relationships.

The men's thinking on the origins of their troubles was dominated by two considerations: work-related problems and physical illness. Jonathan Whiting, for example, described an accident at work which caused multiple fractures:

> 'I was off sick for nearly a year. When I returned, they didn't give me my job back, they put me into another one, with less money, less everything. I always worked in the factory, on the shop-floor, I want to go back . . . but there is nothing I can do, not with unemployment around . . . besides, I am no good at this job, I am forgetful, I am not a clerk'.

Mr Whiting, given the job of assistant storekeeper, which he did not want, was unable to find employment elsewhere. Industrial accident, involving not himself but someone else, was given as an explanation by Steve Coleman who witnessed a mate being fatally crushed:

> 'He was sucked into the machine. He never had a chance. I couldn't get it out of my mind; I still can't'.

Other men said that work pressures were too much for them, or that the work was too exhausting and they couldn't cope. Two men complained of shift-work, which they had not previously experienced, others feared redundancy and unemployment.

Physical illness was regarded as a cause of nervous troubles, alone or in combination with work problems. A few male respondents said that their problem was 'post-operational depression' which, hospital staff had explained, was quite usual. Others blamed heart conditions, chest problems and orthopaedic problems for their subequent neurosis. Ill-health was frequently linked to work-related difficulties and Jonathan Whiting was not alone in supposing that the one was caused by the other; James Rees explained that following an operation on his back he spent some time in an orthopaedic ward and suffered from post-operative depression. This turned into long-term depression when he learned that he could not go back to his previous employment because he was no longer suited to heavy work. He repeatedly said 'I don't know what else I can do and it wears me down'. Philip Woods, who after 25 years' employment at the same factory, was put on shift-work, said that the change caused his health to deteriorate: he could not adjust to the irregular sleep pattern, not cope with the switch of meal times; he complained of digestive upsets, loss of weight and lack of sleep.

Hardly any of the men appeared to have explored their own past actions as possible causes, but four mentioned adverse life events as possible contributory factors. One had been 'taken to Court by the Social Security' for not declaring his earnings and said that this upset him so much that he took an overdose; another reported trouble with the police over stolen goods, at a time when he was much disturbed by a death in the family.

Perhaps the most striking difference between the women and the men was that the women tended not to accept the 'obvious' explanation of their misfortunes and continued to search for the meaning of their experiences whereas the men, having come up with an explanation, were content to stay with it.

THE FEAR OF GOING MAD

The struggle to make sense of experiences, which typically followed their being named as 'psychiatric patients', was accompanied by the need to face up to a most threatening possibility, that of going mad. Psychiatric practice is closely linked with madness in popular image and to many people referral to a psychiatrist implies the possibility of madness, in spite of doctors' assurances that this is not the case.

Madness, the state of 'losing one's mind' is one of the most frightening of fates and people who feel themselves threatened regard it with extreme fear. As Goffman observed, losing one's mind is 'the most pervasively threatening thing that can happen to the self in our society' (Goffman, 1961).

Not everyone considered this possibility; to some, psychiatric treatment implied a minor and much less threatening condition than the extreme form. But those who did consider the possibility certainly did so with fear and alarm.

May, 54, no children: 'When my doctor first said, go to a psychiatrist, I felt terrified that it means I am going mad. I hated going there, I thought it could mean, I will end up being mad'.

Mavis, 34, one child 10: 'I was simply terrified when I was sent to the psychiatrist. I thought "I don't want to see those mentally ill people, I don't want to end up like them, am I really as bad as that? I must be if I am sent there"'.

Mandy, 24, three children 4, 6 and 8: 'I thought it meant that I was going nuts. I couldn't bear the thought that I'm as bad as that. Even now I've started to go [to the psychiatrist] I ask Sid [husband] 'do you think I'm going mad'?

The reaction of those who felt themselves to be so threatened could be paraphrased thus: 'Although I feel completely sane, the doctor knows the signs, if he sends me to a psychiatrist, I must be going mad'. The terrifying prospect of madness, once faced, served to reduce further a self-confidence already at a low ebb.

3 Women, Work and Neurosis

There is a complex reciprocal relationship between health and work. Health can be affected by work and by the lack of it; ill-health can reduce both the ability and the desire to work. Industrial societies traditionally have placed considerable emphasis on the moral value of work both to the individual and to the community, and to the extent that the sick and impaired are unable to work not only their afflictions but, by extension, they themselves have been deemed unfortunate and undesirable. Studies of people suffering from ill-health or impairment have shown how stigma, job problems, unemployment and downward social mobility affect their lives (Blaxter, 1976), whilst studies of unemployment reveal health problems consequent upon lack of work (Harrison, 1983). Thus, ill-health can be both cause and consequence of not working, and sick, unemployed people come to be viewed as social problems.

Within the wider complexities of the work-health relationship there lie the special problems of women and the ways in which their lives are affected both by domestic and by outside employment. Traditionally, the workplace of women was in the home but the work done there was, and still is for that matter, deemed 'non-work', being unwaged labour. One of the great social revolutions of this century has been the mass entry of married women into the labour market. This is not the place to discuss the reasons for this development; suffice it to say that two-income families are everywhere to be met with as wives pursue careers of their own.

Nonetheless, these women also continue their unpaid work in

the home, domestic chores and childcare still being regarded unequivocally (and not least by themselves) as the duty of women.

In Britain, almost 60 per cent of married women were working in paid employment in the early 1980s (General Household Survey for 1980 and 1981). The majority of mothers with children over 5 years of age were employed (67 per cent) and so were a substantial minority of mothers with children under five (30 per cent). Most of these mothers, as indeed the majority of married women in employment, were engaged in part-time work.

Studies comparing the relative situations of women in paid employment with those engaged solely in domestic work, contrasting their relative economic and social positions, their self-esteem and their power, have adduced evidence which points decidedly to the better situation of the wage earners. Even so, there continues to prevail an ambivalent attitude to women in paid employment, especially married women with children. Unlike men, who are accepted and valued if they work and criticised and devalued if they do not, women come in for criticism on both counts. Employment is deemed inimical to domestic work and childcare which, in turn, are seen as distractions affecting women's performance as employees. It is hardly surprising that many women suffer from the duality of the demands made upon them.

Table 3.1: Employment status of women diagnosed as neurotic

| | First interview | | Second interview | |
	Nos	%	*Nos*	%
Full-time housewife	48	74*	43	66*
Full-time paid employment	7	11	10	15
Part-time paid employment	10	15	12	19
Total	65	100	65	100

*Includes women who did paid work for 4 hours per week or less.

It will be apparent from Table 3.1 that the women of the survey were untypical in that the majority of them were full-time housewives. In this chapter, the relationship between the work of women (both domestic and waged) and their neurotic problems, will be considered.

DOMESTIC WORK AND NEUROSIS

The stresses inherent in domestic work and the role of the housewife can lead to neurosis which in its turn is likely to make her even more home-centred and thus vulnerable to further stress. Moreover, excessive housework itself can be a form of adjustment to intolerable demands, a response called by doctors 'neurotic'. So, the home can become, for the full-time housewife, a setting which, by its peculiar strains, 'drives her mad' yet which provides asylum from the impossible demands of the world outside with which she feels that she can no longer cope.

In the last two decades, the notion of stress in daily life and its consequences for physical and mental well-being have been explored. A causal sequence has been argued according to which stresses may trigger or cause psychological problems (Brown and Harris, 1978; Verbrugge, 1984). Occupational stress has been identified in many different kinds of employment; police, school-teachers, executives, health workers and many others are exposed to stresses attendant upon the nature of their work (Chavkin, 1984). Housework is not alone in having its built-in stresses; it is, however, peculiar in that it bears a stress-free image—very different from the reality.

The most frequently found sources of stress in housewives are the long working hours, monotony and an absence of rules, combined with isolation, confinement and a heavy measure of responsibility (Oakley, 1974; Chavkin, 1984; Sharpe, 1984). The working hours of many housewives far exceed those prevailing in other occupations. According to Ann Oakley, for housewives in Britain, 77 hours is the average length of the working week, a stint which would be utterly unacceptable to workers in other occupations, for whom there is a scheduled end to the day's work, a time when they can walk out of the factory gates or close work, a time when they can walk out of the factory gates or close the office door behind them. Not so for the housewife, for whom the job has no end, no moment when she can relax with the feeling of a job well done but rather the self-reproach that there is always something else needing her attention. It is hardly to be wondered at that the unrelenting demands of housework and its interminable nature are productive of stress in women. Nor is that all: unlike the situation in other workplaces, there are no clear rules or standards, no job description and neither supervision nor guidance. To work under such conditions may, superficially, seem attractive, but an absence of rules can as well result in doing too much as too little. Working without structure is far from easy, as students, writers and the self-employed can testify; one has to build the structure and allocate the appropriate number of hours to each task only to find, all too frequently, that while the number of hours in a day is limited, the volume of work is not. For the housewife, to the stress of the potentially unending nature of her duties is added the uncertainties of whether the work has been done well or badly. The same household tasks can be done by different women in one hour or six (Friedan, 1963) and it is not easy for the housewife to assess the length of time that she should devote to any one task; the only yardstick she can employ is the cleanliness and appearance of her home compared with those of other women in similar social and financial circumstances.

The attraction of housework is often said to be its autonomy, the freedom to organise one's day and the feeling that 'you are your own boss'. This was given as the most valued feature of being a housewife in Ann Oakley's study on housework (1974). Autonomy was not so much positively valued by her respondents as regarded as a preferable alternative to disliked employment pressures: 'you don't have to get up early in the morning to go out to work, there is nobody behind you with a punchcard' (p. 42). However, the freedom to organise one's day is often illusory in practice. There is no supervisor, but there are tasks which relentlessly have to be done at a certain time every day and which shape the daily work schedule. Children have to be escorted to and from school, meals for the family need to be prepared on time, babies demand set routines, meals and medication for sick people in the household have to be fitted into the work schedule. The 'autonomous' housewife soon finds that she has to get up early and that the punchcard is no less real for not being there beside the clock.

The large measure of responsibility attaching to the care of other members of the family is another stressful feature of the work of housewives. Caring for the young and old, home nursing and bringing up children are aspects of domestic work which are increasingly dominated by health professionals, who advise, regulate and demand, in the name of professionally approved standards to which housewives and mothers are required to adhere. Housewives are told that they are responsible for the lives and well-being of their families. Indeed, women's responsibility for the health of the family has received more and more emphasis in the present century, as public health issues have been brought into the forefront of public consciousness, following on the promulgation of the germ theory of disease. As Oakley argues. 'Pasteur's discovery had the advantage that disease could be reclassified as in principle under man's control—or, more specifically, as controllable by means of the cleanliness and commonsense of women' (Oakley, 1981B, p. 178). Dirt in the home has come to be regarded as a potential source of disease, and housewives have assumed responsibility for the prevention of sickness, by eliminating germs.

Increasing emphasis on the quality of family life and new standards of childcare have placed added burdens on women. Mothers are blamed for the psychological as well as the physical problems of their children, as 'caring' professionals join health workers in advice-giving. Too much interference as well as deprivation can be cited, as mothers are held responsible for the conduct, happiness and quality of life of their children (Doyal, 1979).

Thus, research findings have demonstrated the many stressful features of housework which nevertheless continues to bear a stress-free image. Moreover, the stress of the work itself is only one of the disagreeable aspects of housework; its under-valuing by society, the lack of recognition of the problems involved and its image as unskilled work requiring no training, all contribute to the low status accorded to the women engaged in full-time domestic work. Low status leads to low self-esteem, the 'I am only a housewife' feeling, and to lack of confidence in one's ability to achieve more in an achievement orientated society (Gavron, 1966; Sharpe, 1984). The fact that housework is unpaid and that full-time housewives are economically dependent on their wage-earning husbands, buttresses these feelings of low status and inadequacy.

Given its negative aspect it is hardly surprising that so many housewives feel dissatisfied with their position. Prolonged dissatisfaction and unhappiness, combined with a sense of the hopelessness of finding an acceptable and viable solution, are widespread among housewives. These feelings were shared by the women in the survey who were engaged in full-time, or near full-time domestic duties; they described housework as monotonous, demanding and never-ending, a job with much responsibility and little recognition.

Nevertheless, the notion that the stresses of their position as housewives may have led to their neurotic problems was an entirely alien thought which hardly ever came to these women. The findings of sociological studies on housework and the writings of feminist authors on housewives never reached them. Although the problems of housewives have been publicised in women's magazines, radio programmes etc. in recent years, so also have other messages concerning the essentially happy and contented nature of housewives and mothers (see TV advertisements for detergents and nappies for example). These latter messages may well prove the stronger confirming, as they do, the traditional cultural image of women as wives and mothers. To most of the women in the survey, neurosis was connected with their role as housewives only insofar as it hampered the performance of their domestic duties. It was only extreme hardship that caused a few of them to think through their situation and to speculate that the exigencies of these duties might have brought on their neurotic problems.

From the ways that these women spoke about their domestic role, certain mechanisms connecting housework and particular forms of neurosis became apparent. Firstly, the unending nature of the job, combined with its heavy demands, was linked with depression; secondly, how best to carry out the manifold responsibilities for family health and well-being gave rise to anxiety; thirdly, absence of rules and of standards was linked with obsessive concern for cleanliness. It is not argued here that these particular aspects of housework are, by themselves, causes of particular neurotic problems, nor that women who do not experience these pressures cannot develop similar problems. Rather, the argument is that certain stresses inherent in housework may well contribute to emotional states which are deemed to be 'neurotic' and that certain features of housework can shape the form that neurosis takes.

The connection between long hours, never-ending work and depression was expressed clearly by June and Julie, who were diagnosed as suffering from that condition:

June 35, four children 2, 8, 13 and 16: 'The worst part of it is, there is never an end to it. I get up at six every morning, that's alright, I don't mind that, I am fresh then. By lunch time I am always tired, but the day goes on, Annie has to be fetched from the bus, then the boys come home, then my husband . . . meals, washing up, and the baby is there all the time . . . when I go to bed at night, I think of all the things I wanted to do, the ironing still not done, I didn't take the boys' shoes to the repair . . . there is no end and I work and work and nothing is done . . . I feel depressed at night, I don't know how to face the next day, some nights I say to myself, I will not get up next morning, what is the point of it all'?

Julie 30, two children 5 and 7: 'I think it was coping with the children and the house that started my depression. The boys are too active, too boisterous, need attention all the time, I can't control them. The work is never ending. I clean the room, the boys make it a mess in five minutes . . . I cook and shop and clean . . . I mean, if I could finish once, have an evening when I can say, it's all done, I can relax, but it never happens. My husband comes home, he's finished his work, I never finish mine. I get more depressed and tired as the day goes on'.

While the tiring and unending nature of housework has received attention in recent years, the increasing responsibilities for the health and well-being of their families, which have been placed on housewives, and the blame they receive from health and welfare professionals when anything goes wrong, have been less explored. Yvonne and Rita were diagnosed as suffering from anxiety neurosis.

Yvonne 35, three children 2, 9 and 11 (the middle child was adopted): 'When I had two miscarriages the doctors said it was my fault. He was very nice about it, but he said it was best to tell me what I am doing wrong, so that I can try to change. He said I worked too much, didn't eat the right food and, it's a bit embarrassing, but he said maybe I don't keep myself clean enough and infection gets in. When I had the third miscarriage, I knew it was no good and we adopted Joanna. The health visitor and the social worker came nearly every day, you know how careful thay have to be with an adopted child, they told me what to do but I was getting more and more worried . . .. The social worker kept on telling me how I should treat the two children, so that Joanna doesn't become jealous and a problem child . . . I was getting quite anxious I felt everybody depended on me doing it right and I couldn't stop worrying. We settled down again while the baby was on the way, but after that I got more and more anxious . . . am I doing it right? . . . is everything clean? . . . is everybody happy? I can't stop being anxious and worried when so much depends on me'.

Rita 27, two children 2½ and 5½: 'I had a breakdown last spring, soon after the children were better. It's funny to say this, but this is what happened. Annabelle just started school and had whooping cough. My doctor said I must be careful with the baby but he caught it too . . . I can't tell you how worried I was and how I blamed myself. I decided earlier not to have them vaccinated and when they caught it I thought it is all my fault. I was sick with worry . . . I thought I should have managed it so that the baby doesn't catch it . . . then they were better and after two weeks the little one started gastroenteritis . . . I was sure it happened because I didn't clean the house enough when they had whooping cough . . . I was so worried, then Annabelle went back to school, the baby was alright again and I went down with this breakdown. The doctor said I was wrong worrying so much, I was too tense and anxious'.

As discussed earlier, many people tend to self-blame, not only for their own sickness but for that of other members of the family; it is part of making sense of things that happen to them and of understanding their environment and their lives. The women of the survey experienced this sense of guilt for sickness when it occurred and were not helped by health workers pointing out their shortcomings, nor by doctors telling them that worrying too much about such things amounted to anxiety neurosis.

Responsibility for health has implications for cleanliness in the home, but lack of established standards is stressful in that it can lead to ever more efforts to get things clean. The women who talked about their 'obsessions' with cleanliness and high standards of housework said that they 'didn't know when to stop'. The feeling that they had to do better and better grew until nothing else mattered.

> *Ruth 48, one grown-up son:* 'I feel I have to go on as if somebody was driving me. I clean the sink six or seven times a day, and even then I fancy that there is dirt on it . . . . When I go to visit my mother or my sister I just set to and clean their kitchen . . . . My mother said not to do it, when I cleaned her oven, she was quite annoyed, but I can't stop myself'.

Unlike Yvonne and Rita, who blamed themselves and were not surprised to receive censure from health workers, Ruth at first expected praise from everyone for her excellence as a housewife and was surprised and hurt when she did not receive it. Others too were taken aback when their doctors told them that they were too houseproud and that cleaning had become an obsession.

Housewives who want to compete, achieve and excel in a society where competition and achievement are important values, have to operate in the private domain of home and family. High standards of housework and childcare constitute the only kind of excellence they can aim at.

It is, unfortunately, no more possible to establish a clear borderline between normal and obsessive amounts of housework than it is to distinguish clearly between normal concern for the health of the family and neurotic anxiety over it.

Health itself is difficult to define and the dividing line between it and illness is notoriously difficult to establish (Miles, 1978). It is all too easy to do ever more housework, to worry increasingly over one's responsibilities and to get just that little more depressed day by day until suddenly one finds oneself labelled neurotic.

PRESSURE TO STAY AT HOME

By the time of the second interview, one year after their referral for psychiatric treatment, only five out of the forty-eight non-working housewives had some paid employment and a further two had actively sought work. A few others said that they had looked for work in a half-hearted way, scanning the papers and so on in case some 'small ideal employment' presented itself. Thus, forty-eight women (66 per cent) were still wholly engaged in domestic work and it seems likely that at least some of them could have found work had they really tried; they were certainly dissatisfied with being 'just housewives'. Why did they not try to change their status?

The answer is complex. Firstly, the women were subject to pressures, familiar to married women generally, to stay at home; secondly, they experienced, or at any rate perceived, constraints placed upon them by their neurotic problems. Pressures of the first kind were manifold: many of the women's lives were so dominated by the demands of husband and children that the idea of an alternative life-style in which their own needs could find proper expression hardly occurred to them. Typically, the mothers of young children felt that the prospect of work outside the home was not open to them, others, caring for disabled husband, sick child, etc. felt that these obligations defined the home as the only possible place for them to be.

It has been remarked that the traditional notion of 'woman's place' being in the home and her role that of caring for the family, can be so strongly internalised in women that any alternatives may be rejected without consideration (Friedan, 1963; Barrett, 1979). Recent research on the 'caring' function of women has argued that there are powerful ideological and material forces in present-day society which determine that women, rather than men, undertake the informal caring for dependent people (Ungerson, 1983; Baldwin and Glendenning, 1983). In this research, the women respondents were in an even weaker position than usual when it came to resisting pressures and contemplating changes, so much so that even those without children or other dependents stayed at home as housewives. One reason was that low self-esteem and lack of self-confidence were felt with heightened intensity by women who had been labelled neurotic.

Low self-esteem and loss of confidence affect housewives in general, as researchers have demonstrated. Women who have not worked outside their homes for many years tend to lose confidence in their ability to find work. Writing about mothers of young children, Sue Sharpe says that

Being separate from the work outside can erode the ability to meet and talk to new people. Self-assurance may slip away as the experience of working recedes. As time goes by, the prospect of going back to work seems rather remote and unattainable. Job interviews appear as terrifying ordeals, especially with no immediate job experience to lean on. (1984, p. 35)

Women receiving psychiatric treatment have even less confidence.

Jane 55, one married son: 'I didn't work when I was younger and it's too late now. I have no qualifications, no experience, there is no point looking, at my age. I look at the papers sometimes, just out of interest, and see vacancies, then I think who would want me? I work in my garden a lot, and decorate the house instead'.

Alice 33, no children: 'I am not qualified to do anything. I missed the boat as far as work is concerned. I didn't work when I got married, I thought that children would come along. Then I had tests [for infertility] and the years went by . . . I have no work experience, I couldn't find work'.

Women who have been labelled neurotic have to battle with self-abasement to an even greater extent than do housewives generally because implicit in the label attached to them is the judgement that they are inadequate, problematic and have been found wanting in some way. Jane's sentiment 'who would want me'? was echoed by others.

A reason for some housewives not seeking outside employment is that their husbands prefer them to stay at home. Researchers have found that although a substantial minority of husbands encourage their wives to have paid employment there are many who disapprove and some whose view is that they don't mind 'as long as they [the wives] could cope and the family did not suffer' (Sharpe, 1984, p. 167). Husbands of employed women continue to regard housework and childcare largely as women's work and their own role in such matters as, at best, one of helping out (Land, 1983; Graham, 1984). Even men who profess not to mind their wives working may behave in a manner which conveys the opposite. Certainly there were several housewives in the survey who said that their husbands liked them to stay at home; others described difficulties which clearly showed their husband's preference for them to do so.

Alice, (again): 'My husband doesn't want me to work anyway. He is at home one week in every three and likes me to be there. He wants all attention to himself'.

Edna, 49, 2 children 17 and 19: 'We would need another car if I went out to work and my husband says it would be far too expensive. He doesn't think it would be worth it'.

Lisa, 31, 3 children 3, 7 and 9: 'My husband is on shifts and when he is at home it is important that I should be there. He works very hard and the change from days to nights upsets him, he wants me at home to give him his meals. Maybe when he is not on shifts anymore he will not mind if I am not there'.

Thus, housewives with neurotic problems have numerous pressures on them to stay at home. The traditional expectation that primarily they should be housewives combines with low self-esteem and loss of confidence to inhibit effective search for employment. They share these pressures with married women in general, but once the label 'neurotic' is applied, their already weak position is further undermined to the point where they are unable to resist them. Their self-confidence, already at a low ebb, is further diminished by the label, and beset by doubts and questioning their own competence and judgement, they are ever less able to oppose traditional expectations and assumptions.

In addition to pressures shared with housewives in general, those in the sample experienced particular constraints placed on them by specific neurotic problems, which prevented them from leaving their homes and seeking paid employment. Their situation was forcefully expressed by the agoraphobic housewives. Agoraphobia is a morbid fear of public places and more than one of the women suffering from it expressed the fear that she would 'make a fool of herself' outside the home. Agoraphobic housewives spoke of their panic attacks in public places and said that their condition prevented them from leaving their homes at all (at least, unaccompanied) let alone seeking work outside, however much they would like it.

Sufferers from depression felt constraints of a different kind; they were too low, too exhausted, and too imbued with a sense of hopelessness even to start looking for a job, much less actually to take one. To these women their domestic duties were already more than they could manage, they couldn't cope with the children and the housework, let alone assume another responsibility. This despairing attitude was shared by women who suffered from eating disorders or anxiety states.

Of course the way that a problem is formulated influences the solutions sought for it; if the problem is seen to be a failure to cope with housework and children, because of some inner insufficiency, or lack of stamina, or inability to organise oneself, then employment outside the home is not considered as a solution at all, rather an impossible burden. Only if the problem is reformulated as dissatisfaction with the conditions and stresses of domestic work can employment be seen as a solution.

Among the housewives were some who said that they had actually lost their previous employment because of depression or agoraphobia and that they must fully recover before looking for paid work again. Indeed, to the women who were interested in employment at all, the situation appeared quite straightforward: first conquer your agoraphobia, or depression or anxiety, then look for work outside.

Interestingly, abandonment of paid employment was seen by a few of the women as a possible remedy for their neurotic problems, a view encouraged in some cases by family doctors. However, hopes that staying at home would bring about an improvement proved unavailing.

> *Brenda 34, three children 3, 5 and 9:* 'I worked part time in a restaurant, every lunchtime for a year when my youngest was 18 months old. I lost the job when I became depressed. I was very low and I stayed at home . . . the doctor said maybe staying at home would help, I was taking tablets as well . . . I thought there would be less pressure, more time to clean the house . . . after a time I felt worse, more depressed . . . I felt shut in, alone with the children. I don't know what to do now, I can't work, feeling so depressed, I haven't the energy to look for work . . . I am getting worse staying at home'.

Helen Roberts, in research concerned with middle-aged women patients and their doctors, also found an inclination among doctors to suggest to women, grappling with the dual demands of home and outside employment, that the latter should be given up.

'The doctors with whom we came into contact linked some of the problems of the menopause and of other illnesses of women in their middle years, with stress and overwork. But the solution which they tended to suggest was that women should give up work—meaning paid work outside the home, this being the only category of work they seemed to acknowledge'. (Roberts, 1985, p. 64).

It might be thought that women who would have liked to enter into paid employment and yet felt unable to do so were more severely affected by neurotic problems than those who had such employment. However, there was nothing to show, either from the interviews or in the records that this was the case.

PAID EMPLOYMENT

At the time of the second interviews, twenty-two of the women were in full or part-time paid employment.

The employment pattern of women with neurotic problems is qualitatively inferior to that of employed women generally; the constraints are greater and the opportunities, more limited.

Most of the twenty-two women were unskilled workers and all of them were employed in the service sector.

Table 3.2: Occupation of women respondents

	Full-time	Part-time
Home help	—	2
Hospital worker (in laundry or cleaning)	—	3
School helper (meals)	—	2
Shop assistant	3	1
Secretary	2	2
Hairdresser	—	1
Nurse	2	1
Canteen or kitchen help	3	—
Total	10	12

In addition, eight women who worked for fewer than four hours per week, and therefore were regarded essentially as housewives, had similar sorts of employment; four were home helps, three did a little home typing and one helped with school meals. Likewise, the two housewives who had actively looked for a job had tried in the service area.

The main constraint on the employment possibilities of these women was the perceived need to work locally. Nearly all of them worked close to home, having set out to find the nearest possible employer. This need for local work arose from two main causes: the necessity of combining paid employment with domestic responsibilities, and the special problems posed by their neurotic condition.

Of course, most working mothers with young children face difficulties in trying to combine employment with housework and childcare and they usually find that a job near home, preferably one with flexible hours, best serves this requirement (Sharpe, 1984). Additional problems for respondents were posed by their having to attend treatment sessions during working hours and, from time to time, by their being too depressed, or distressed to go to work.

For agoraphobics, travelling on public transport was an ordeal, and some of the depressives also could not contemplate working more than a short distance from home. There were women with other phobias who could not work in rooms without windows, or in basements, while others could not face open-plan offices.

Marion, 33, three children 9, 10 and 13: works in hospital laundry 16 hours per week. 'I was lucky I found this job, four mornings a week, it fits in with the children and I can go to treatment as well. My boss is not very sympathetic, but she can't be, the hospital wouldn't allow it. They are very strict on time-keeping. But I am lucky to have work, I couldn't go very far of course, the hospital is just round the corner . . .. Four mornings works out well for us'.

Beryl, 33, twins aged 9: works as home help and assists with school meals. 'I've worked for the same family for the last two years. I go there twice a week, it's easy because no one is at home, they are all out at business. I also put my name down at the school to do school meals but had to wait for years, there is always a waiting list. The school is just round the corner, and the family live in the street next to it. I couldn't travel in a bus, it has to be local work for me'.

Sandra, 32, two children 6 and 13: works in a department store as a waitress every lunchtime. 'I had a terrible time trying to find work. I had a part-time job, two full days, Saturday and Sunday, as supervisor of an office cleaning firm. It didn't work out because my husband refused to have the children every weekend. I tried to leave them with my parents but that didn't work, so I had to give up the job. I just couldn't find another local job, the only one I found was at the hospital but that was every afternoon and I had to go to therapy then. Finally, I was lucky, my sister works at the Store and heard of the vacancy for a lunchtime waitress. She takes me there every day and I come back on the bus, it is only two stops and I am back by half three'.

Women in general find in the service sector (meaning, of course, catering, cleaning, small shops etc.) work that can be done (indeed, for them, has to be done) part-time, at odd hours, and thus can be fitted in with domestic duties. Sue Sharpe found that working mothers were typically looking for a 'convenient job':

when mothers return to work they often set their own talents or inclinations to one side and take the most convenient job they can find to suit their family situation . . . . With a dependent family to care for, factors like hours and locality take precedence over the nature of a job, its rate of pay, status and prospects. (Sharpe, 1984, p. 51)

Mothers of young children are by no means the only group of people, both able and wanting to work, who can take employment only if flexible working arrangements can be provided for them; women caring for sick and disabled relatives, and the disabled themselves are among others in this category. Employers who are prepared to make special arrangements are much sought after by these groups even if pay and conditions are not always all they could be. Frequently, such employers are small firms or private individuals.

Frances, 40, no children: full-time shop assistant in a small newsagent/supermarket. 'It is a small shop, open very long hours and the owner is very good. When I had to go to group therapy in the afternoons, we agreed that I make it up on Sunday mornings. One week I couldn't work at all, but the week after, I went in early mornings as well. Not every employer would agree to that'.

Writing of working mothers, Sue Sharpe (1984) also found that individual bargains were made by women with employers for the period of school holidays or when sick children needed attention.

'These individual bargains are attractive to women because they offer informal and flexible conditions within a personal relationship. Such an arrangement has a familiar paternalistic quality, and is usually between a male employer and a female employee. The personal touch is especially significant because in developing feminine identity, women internalise the importance of people and relationships and look for them in the workplace'. (p. 62)

Women with neurotic illnesses often have to accept lesser jobs than those they previously held. Beryl had been a trained and experienced secretary but suffered intermittent unemployment, first, because she had to stay at home with the twins, and then because her agoraphobia prohibited journeys on public transport. Sandra had trained as a hairdresser and worked in a high-class establishment before her second child was born after which, struggling with depression, she became a waitress. Liz had a responsible hospital job, specialising in ophthalmic nursing, prior to her breakdown.

Liz, 29, no children: 'I work in a private Home for old people now. They don't need much nursing. I always take the night shift, it is undemanding work, I just have to be there but usually there is little to do. It is not the work I would have chosen before the breakdown but I am lucky to have it. I couldn't cope with demanding work and in any case I couldn't get a hospital job now. The Home is very near, I walk across the park and I am there'.

Downward mobility also characterises the employment pattern of mothers returning to work when their children are older (Sharpe, 1984) and is part of life for the suddenly disabled seeking employment (Blaxter, 1976). These groups share the difficulties of reduced employment opportunities and the pattern is all too often one of taking the 'convenient job' sliding into a situation of lower pay and no prospects, as hours, suitability and location take precedence over other conditions of work. For the women in the survey, 'convenient' employment opportunities were extremely limited which is why many felt 'lucky' to have work at all. Some would have changed their employment if it were not for their neurotic problems and others said they would do so if it were not for the children. They looked forward to a future when their children were older and their neurosis gone.

It was interesting to find that most of the employed women had a work identity closely related to their domestic role. Work as a 'home-help' means cleaning someone else's home as well as your own; working in a hospital laundry, giving lunches to young children at school, and working in a restaurant kitchen, are all jobs closely related to the domestic role of housewives and requiring the same domestic skills. Paid employment is usually regarded by sociologists as belonging to the public domain and unpaid domestic work to the private domain (Garmanikov *et al.,* 1983A). But the public-private dichotomy is not easily applicable to the work of many women, nor is it always a useful tool in analysing women's situation. The 'public' employment of many women in the survey was essentially located in the private domain of home and childcare and constituted an extension of the traditional female role.

However, even if located in the vicinity of home, even if only an extension of housework, outside employment provides a means of getting out of the house. That, and the extra money, were the aspects of it that mattered most to many of the women. Going out to work may provide an opportunity of adult companionship (the importance of which is discussed in the next chapter) and an incentive to pay attention to dress, hair and make-up, all too easily neglected when habitually seen only by members of the family. With depression comes loss of pride and an increasing neglect of one's personal appearance. For women, to look good is to feel good and those suffering from depression who obtained jobs, found that smartening themselves up made them feel better.

> *Sandra* (again): 'I have to look smart, hair done and everything, if I want to keep my job. At first I had to make a tremendous effort, my sister dragged me to the hairdresser, but now I enjoy it and I don't feel so depressed when I look in the mirror'.

Research in recent years has demonstrated that paid employment functions as a protection for women against psychological disorders (Brown and Harris, 1978). Sue Sharpe found that mothers of young children felt better, more confident, less depressed when they returned to work, and in a study of tranquilliser users it was shown that women who were able to return to work had less need of these drugs (Cooperstock and Lennard, 1979).

FEELING GUILTY

A striking feature of the women's attitudes to housework was the strong guilt feeling they showed for disliking it. Of course, guilt feeling is characteristic of women's lives in general, and it is not peculiar to psychiatric patients. Many full-time housewives and mothers who are dissatisfied and unhappy at home consequently feel guilty. Sue Sharpe argues that 'women learn their social role and develop their feminine identity in the course of growing up and identifying with their own mothers and other women. In so doing they generally take on a strong sense of responsibility for the home and for children. Domestic family life and motherhood is supposed to provide them with a satisfying role, so if instead it makes them frustrated and unhappy, they are left with conflicting feelings and guilt. These are exacerbated if husbands, relatives and friends also assume that they should be happy and fulfilled' (Sharpe, 1984, p. 37).

Advertising, especially, constantly reaffirms the message that housewives and mothers should be happy and contented (Millum, 1975). They are portrayed smiling, well-dressed, not a hair out of place, positively enjoying such mundane tasks as washing up and floor cleaning, all made simple by the use of this or that product. It is no wonder that the woman failing to cope, irritable with the children and generally unhappy, feels blameworthy. Added to this guilt feeling is a reluctance to express dissatisfaction or to state preferences which go against traditional role expectations. Indeed, the study of tranquilliser users, mentioned above, reported that many women experienced this kind of strain (Cooperstock and Lennard, 1979, p. 340).

Female psychiatric patients are liable to experience the disapproval of another powerful agency, the doctors, who frequently reinforce their guilt feelings and encourage their notions that something must be wrong within themselves. Doctors often convey the diagnostic label of neurosis as a sign of disapproval, and by so doing enhance guilt. Leeson and Gray argue that, in effect, doctors say 'You have a lovely home, a good husband and two beautiful children, everything a woman could want and you are not satisfied. You must be neurotic' (1978, p. 162).

During the interviews, housewives frequently remarked that they could not be 'normal' women if, having such comfortable homes, they were depressed, anxious or 'nervy' and that they must be unnatural mothers for not being happy and contented with their children.

Mandy 24, three children 4, 6 and 8, and a new-born baby: 'Some days I feel I can't go on. I force myself to get up and feed the baby and get the children off to school. I drag myself and I know I look terrible . . . I look at other mothers, they seem dressed up and smiling and I wonder how they manage . . . It is not only since the baby was born, I was tired and worn out before that too . . . I often think the children would be better without me . . . I must be an unnatural mother, I can't enjoy my children'.

Wendy 27, two children 5 and 7: 'My miscarriage was a punishment for being so miserable at home when I have two healthy, good children. I know I shouldn't feel so weepy and low, the doctor said I have no reason to feel like that and he is right. The other day Paul said "why don't you ever play with us Mummy, like Richard's Mum"? . . . I know I am not a good companion . . . . My husband says the same, I never want to go out now'.

That their neurotic problems might have a damaging effect upon their children was, clearly, another matter over which young mothers felt guilty. Agoraphobics, in particular, fretted over not being able to take them to school or attend parent-teacher meetings; they could not go with the children to parks and playgrounds. They blamed themselves for not shopping well and economically (this was especially true of those for whom supermarkets were large public places, to be feared) and were convinced that the quality of family life was adversely affected by their condition, and that they alone were to blame.

It was of interest to find that guilt-feelings over being unhappy were expressed more cogently by the younger woman. It was not that the older ones were any less discontented, but they may have 'learned to live with it' to some extent and, as their children grew up and left home they could find, in the diminution of their roles as mothers and housekeepers, a socially acceptable reason for their discontent, which assuaged feelings of guilt. They were able to feel that their unhappiness was natural and even deserving of some sympathy whereas the young mothers regarded their discontent as unnatural and unacceptable. It has been shown that doctors encourage middle-aged women to attribute menopausal and other problems to 'emptying the nest'. However false this may be it seems to have the beneficial effect of reducing guilt.

Guilt-feelings were not confined to the women who stayed at home. The employed women experienced the same guilt over their inadequacies as wives and mothers with an added sense of the wrongness of leaving their children in order to go out to work.

In contemporary society it is often asserted that mothers should stay at home with their children, at least for the first few years; that a good mother is a full-time mother.

Women with paid employment are in a double-bind situation. Doyal argues that 'they are assumed to be less effective mothers because their work interferes with their mothering, and less effective workers because their responsibilities as mothers interfere with their work' (Doyal, 1979, p. 217).

To find married women 'feeling guilty' over working in paid employment, when so many of them do just that, was not altogether to be expected. Possibly, the attitudes of non-employed women of the older generation are influential, as notions of femininity are passed from mothers to daughters. Many of the employed mothers in this survey were apprehensive concerning the possible harm to their children, however hard they tried to find a convenient job with suitable hours. For example Sandra, commenting on her earlier job involving work on Saturdays and Sundays, said:

'I think the girls suffered a lot. Their father didn't want to be with them every weekend and they were too restricted in my parents' home . . . . We never had a proper Sunday dinner or a family outing . . . . They became afraid of the weekend, it isn't right when other children look forward to it . . . I suppose I was afraid that they will become like me, depressed and anxious and going to psychiatrists. When you have all that yourself, you are more afraid for your children'.

Even when she changed from weekend to weekday (lunchtime) working, Sandra continued to be afraid that she could be causing harm, especially to her younger daughter (aged 6).

'I worry about her a lot. When Sara was that age [older daughter aged 13] I used to fetch her from school, I can't do it for this one. I used to bake cakes before, I can't now, with my job, I have no time. It's all the little things that she must be missing'.

Guilt-feelings led women to agonise over the rightness or otherwise of going to work; many sought the advice of their doctors. In any case, once they regarded themselves as neurotic, decisions on this and many other aspects of their lives were taken in the light of their condition. Would this or that course of action aggravate or improve their condition? What would be better for the family?

Janet 47, five children between 10 and 28: works in a restaurant every evening. 'After my breakdown I was at home for nine months. I thought the children would benefit but they didn't, I was bad-tempered and fed-up all the time and irritated by every little thing. I am much happier at home if I can get away from it sometimes. It's no good for the children, having a mother who is all nerves'.

For most of the women guilt-feelings were part of daily life, a burden they had to live with.

4 Stigma: The Experience of Rejection

Are so-called neurotics stigmatised in our society? Are those who receive psychiatric treatment and are seen as mentally disturbed, thereby devalued, discredited and less acceptable to their fellows, becoming in fact 'spoiled' persons, the condition which, according to Goffman, is the essence of stigma? (Goffman, 1961).

The concepts 'mental illness' and 'mental patient' have an unfavourable public image. Numerous studies have demonstrated that stigma is attached to mental illness, that people reject and discriminate against the mentally ill and that these negative attitudes change very slowly, if at all (D'Arcy and Brockman, 1977; Miles, 1987).

There are several reasons for this stigmatisation, perhaps the most important being that social expectations are liable to be interrupted and may even break down following mental illness. Disturbed persons may fail to comply with social norms, may even violate them, and thus they appear unpredictable and inexplicable to their fellows. The consequence of a breakdown in social expectations is the attachment of stigma.

Public attitudes also continue to be coloured by notions of the past management of the severely mentally ill (the 'lunatics' of earlier days). Certainly, up to the mid-1950s, mental illness hospitals were crowded with in-patients, many of them long-staying. Visitors could observe few signs of treatment by doctors, they saw only patients living, more or less permanently, in gloomy over crowded and carefully locked wards; they came away with a feeling of hopelessness concerning the condition. In a quite recent research, the relatives of psychiatric patients being treated in general hospitals were fearful of their being transferred to mental hospitals which they regarded as frightening places (Baruch and Treacher, 1978).

Thus, stigma attaching to severe mental disturbance is strong and it may well be that less severe, 'minor', mental disturbance is viewed by the lay public as akin to the more extreme condition and so carries its stigma. Certainly there exists a strong stereotype of mental illness, or 'madness', associated with violence, weakness and unpredictability, picked up, it is argued, in childhood and constantly reaffirmed by everyday discourse and the mass media (Scheff, 1966). When people hear the term 'mental illness', or one of its numerous colloquial equivalents, they are likely to think of the most bizarre, most unacceptable, forms of the illness. But there is no clear dividing line between the severe and the less severe which can be confused or bracketed together, so that even mild cases may derive 'contamination' by association, and become stigmatised (Field, 1976).

It can be argued, then, that the widespread stigma attaching to mental illness is grounded in ignorance of the nature of the illness, its treatment and prognosis and, indeed, in sheer unfamiliarity with the mentally ill. The hope and expectation of many professionals is that with community care and a wider dissemination of information, understanding and sympathy will replace stigma, even in severe cases. However, there is evidence to the contrary: that even when people are better informed about severe psychiatric problems and their prognosis, stigma remains (Phillips, 1966). Moreover, experience with other stigmatised conditions e.g. the badly burned (Knudson-Cooper, 1981) and the paralysed (Blaxter, 1976) indicates that even when ignorance and unfamiliarity are not factors, stigma persists.

Past studies concerned with public attitudes to mental illness have focused mostly on the experience of severely ill in-patients and ex-patients of mental hospitals; much less attention has been paid to the stigma experience of those with milder forms of emotional and psychological problems who receive psychiatric treatment as out-patients, while continuing to live in the wider community.

Respondents in this research project thought a great deal about stigma but much of their thinking was confused, as was their perception of this social phenomenon as something which might apply to themselves. Feelings of being stigmatised were expressed by men even more forcefully than by women. Indeed, this is the one aspect of the experience of being neurotic which appeared to hit men harder. Male respondents felt that they were ridiculed for developing a condition which is associated in the public mind with women, and that in addition to suffering rejection for being a 'loony', they were laughed at for the particularly feminine form that their condition had taken.

During the interviews there appeared a number of recurrent themes: the expectation of being stigmatised and the consequent fear of testing the likely negative attitudes of others, the actual experience of stigma, the explanations thought up in order to account for negative attitudes and rejection, whether anticipated or experienced, and the decision on how to respond to adverse reactions from others.

ANTICIPATION OF STIGMA

Most respondents were worried that the fact of their having psychiatric treatment would produce negative reactions among their social circle. They anticipated problems, usually in the form of ridicule and derogatory attitudes. This anxiety is understandable and has been demonstrated by several previous studies. In his influential work on stigma, Goffman pointed out that people who acquire stigma later in life, as adults, (contrasting this to the stigma attaching to cogenital conditions) had up to that time shared the attitudes of their social group towards the particular stigmatised condition (Goffman, 1961). In studies of the parents of mentally handicapped children, mothers reported an awareness of the distaste, almost revulsion, that friends, relations and people in the street would feel towards their babies, because they themselves had similarly reacted in the recent past (Edgerton, 1967; Voysey, 1975).

It is not surprising, then, that in the course of discussion respondents attributed to others feelings and attitudes that they themselves had held towards those in their social circle who had undergone psychiatric treatment. Expectations of negative attitudes were most forcefully expressed when discussing the vexed question of whether or not to tell relatives and friends that one is seeing a psychiatrist. Many respondents said that as a general rule they kept quiet about it, telling only those within their immediate social circle. Typical comments were:

'Not many people know'.

'They would think I am nutty if I told them'.

'I don't expect people to understand, best not to say anything'.

Stories of the adverse experiences of people who had talked about their psychiatric treatment to others strengthened the expectation of negative evaluation. For example, John Curzon said that a man had once applied for a job as an electrical fitter to the firm where he himself worked, and had been laughed at by the foreman who interviewed him, on hearing that he suffered from 'anxiety neurosis'. The foreman apparently regarded an adult and, as it happened, well-built man, talking about his anxiety neurosis as a huge joke, to be told in the pub afterwards. The applicant did not get the job. When John Curzon himself started psychiatric treatment (for a quite different problem) he could not bring himself to mention it to anyone, neither friends, relatives nor workmates. He then saw the foregoing incident in a new light and he recalled with some poignancy the way they had all laughed at the idea of a big burly man having an anxiety neurosis.

Kevin Taylor had a vivid memory of his mother being in a mental hospital many years previously, and of his father never visiting or allowing his children to visit her because 'it was so shameful'. Kevin Taylor anticipated humiliating group attitudes and decided not to mention his psychiatric treatment to anyone other than his wife and one close neighbour, a nurse.

Occasionally, personal fears of becoming 'mad' were expressed via the imagined responses of others:

'People would think you are maybe violent and could break out and murder them'.

'If they think I am mad they expect me to become violent, I mean it's reasonable to think that, if you are mad and not yourself—I am afraid of it happening myself'.

Anticipation of stigma, and fear of rejection come easily to someone whose self-esteem is lowered in any case by receiving a psychiatric diagnosis and being told that psychiatric treatment is necessary. Fear of testing anticipated negative evaluation led to many of the respondents concealing the news of their psychiatric treatment from others.

EXPERIENCE OF STIGMA

Not all of those interviewed sought to conceal the fact that they were having psychiatric treatment and few attempted concealment from their close relatives and friends, perhaps because to do so would have been very difficult. But reactions to disclosure were mixed and respondents reported changes in these confidants mostly, although not invariably, for the worse.

It is entirely possible that anticipation of stigma had, at least to some extent, a self-fulfilling quality; that some of those who feared rejection or ridicule wrongly interpreted the responses of others as confirmation of their fears; after all, most people can expect to meet with checks and disappointments from time to time. However, this explanation does not account for the painful surprise that some respondents apparently experienced when certain persons, expected to be sympathetic, reacted negatively; nor for the astonishment of those who had not anticipated stigma and then were faced with it.

Some spoke of a change in group behaviour generally, without citing particular incidents and individuals, feeling that most people around them behaved in a rejecting, unsympathetic manner:

'My friends don't want to know me any more'.

'They don't feel easy with me now'.

'Life is totally changed, people just turn away'.

'People shy away'.

'My colleagues think I am crazy, I wouldn't go back to work there'.

Other respondents complained specifically of those in their social group who changed towards them, citing incidents to illustrate their experiences. Individuals, or occasionally a set of people, would be picked out as those whose behaviour, if not very different from that of others, especially hurt. For example, Deborah, who lives in a cul-de-sac, was particularly hurt by the change in her neighbours. According to her:

'People were always friendly. Two or three of the women used to drop in for coffee most mornings, and I used to go to them and have a chat. They never come now, just stopped coming, and I can't go to them anyway because I tried once or twice and they said they were just going out. So I stopped trying. What hurts me most is that they stop my husband on the street sometimes to ask him how I am, they don't ask me'.

Yvonne mentioned a close friend whose behaviour was most hurtful:

'She was my friend since school, we were very close, and saw each other all the time. Since I started with the psychiatrist, she has been here only once and even then treated me strangely, she wasn't herself at all'.

Not only friends and neighbours but also family members were mentioned as having responded negatively, with ridicule and rejection:

'My mum has changed, she cannot accept that I am mental. she doesn't want to know'.

'My sister-in-law doesn't want me near her children in case I hurt them or go funny, so I don't go there any more'.

Deborah explained that she used to go to her mother's house every Christmas for a family gathering, but stopped because her sisters made snide remarks about psychiatrists and even her mother asked her not to mention the psychiatric clinic in front of the youngsters. Julie described going to the ruby wedding anniversary of her in-laws:

'They were very unkind and Jack [brother-in-law] laughed at me and said I must be funny in the head if I go to the funny place. I felt humiliated, I felt that under the laughing and joking there was unkindness'.

Studies of the stigma associated with physical illness have found that strong stigmatisation can occur in familial and intimate relationships, because it is here that the problems connected with the illness become most apparent (Hopper, 1981). However, the cultural expectation that families stand by and rally round in times of trouble is very strong ('family' for some respondents included all their relatives, others meant only their blood relations as distinct from in-laws) and consequently rejection and ridicule coming from the family was less expected and, when experienced, was more hurtful than that coming from outsiders.

Several of the respondents had enjoyed a close relationship with someone who might have been expected, through personal experience, to be understanding and helpful. One such was Liz, a nurse, whose close friend Kitty, also a nurse, had trained with her many years previously and professionally knew a great deal about psychiatric illness. Far from being supportive, however, Liz reported that:

'Kitty was worse than anyone: when I told her that the psychiatrist recommended group therapy and I started to attend, she completely abandoned the friendship. She has no time to meet me, never rings, and told me she had made new plans for her holiday'.

Another in this category, Muriel, whose sister had previously received psychiatric treatment for anorexia, at least expected understanding from her, but instead met with rejection; Ann, whose husband worked in a hospital and who thought his colleagues would be sympathetic to her problems found, rather, that they made fun of her.

Helen had expected her niece to be the sort of person to whom she could talk, because 'She has a mongol child and knows what it is like to be stigmatised'.

However, this relative turned out to be unsympathetic, not

wanting to talk to her aunt, but saying, behind her back, that she was another 'middle-aged woman loony'.

These responses rankled the more, coming as they did from persons regarded or selected as the 'wise' to use Goffman's terminology. 'Wise' persons, while not themselves possessing a stigmatising attribute, are acquainted with the lives and problems of the stigmatised and so are expected to be knowledgeable and sympathetic. Thus Liz knew her friend Kitty to be familiar with psychiatric illness and therefore expected her to act with sympathy as a 'wise' person. The colleagues of Ann's husband, Helen's niece, and the anorexic sister, also came into this category because their experiences led respondents to expect that they would be 'wiser' and so more tolerant and understanding than people who lacked previous acquaintance with a stigmatising condition. When such expectations failed to materialise, feelings of disappointment and of being let down were the more acute. Rejection was more profoundly felt when it was not anticipated.

Thus the majority of the respondents referred to negative evaluations, rejection and ridicule from their social groups. A few, however, spoke of changes in their friends and relatives which they saw as positive and helpful. These changes tended to occur in cases where the altered behaviour of the respondent had initially evoked negative reactions from acquaintances which then gave way to more positive attitudes on the realisation that the behaviour was due to a problem for which treatment was being received. Elaine said that depression had made her 'unfriendly-like' and, unaware of her problems, relatives, especially her husband's family, were annoyed and offended. On learning about her depression they changed; 'they became more understanding'. Gwen, who suffered from agoraphobia, said:

> 'My neighbours thought I was a snob before they knew, because I never went out and mixed, but now they understand and are quite nice'.

Studies of non-psychiatric conditions have reported that lay groups may become more sympathetic once they know that instances of unacceptable behaviour are due to illness (Shearer,

1981); that slurred speech and an unsteady walk, for example, are due to multiple sclerosis and not to drinking (Miles, 1979). It is rarer for such a positive re-evaluation to take place when the illness is psychiatric, but the quoted examples show that it can happen.

PRIOR CONTACT WITH PSYCHIATRIC PATIENTS

When experiencing, for the first time, a particular medical problem and coming into contact with the appropriate specialist, people draw on the relevant experiences of their social group. Studies of illness behaviour have frequently demonstrated that expectations are influenced not only by personal past experiences but also by group experience. A woman seeking help for, say, backache, for the first time, would have met others suffering from this condition or have joined in discussions about it and thus be able to anticipate social responses and to form some idea of the probable medical diagnosis and treatment. Furthermore, she would interpret the doctor's advice and the responses of her associates in the light of this prior group experience (Wadsworth, *et al.,* 1971; Blaxter and Patterson, 1982).

In cases of stigmatised illness, group experience would constitute an especially valuable guide but, it has been argued, a less readily available one, people tending to be reticent about matters which they regard as 'shameful' e.g. prison, venereal disease, alcoholism and mental illness. Questioned as to whether they had known, prior to their own referral, any other psychiatric patient, no fewer than two-thirds of the respondents answered in the affirmative. The fact that in recent years the ambit of psychiatry has been widened to encompass conditions which were formerly the province of other agencies (or of none) has, in turn, led many people to regard as 'psychiatric' a variety of conditions and behaviour which they can connect, however loosely, with 'the mind'. That said, three of the respondents knew someone who had suffered from the same condition as themselves, namely, depression. Others cited a wide range of cases thought by them to be 'psychiatric' among them a son who needed child-guidance, a mother's nervous breakdown, an elderly uncle who chased little girls, a brother in the Navy who drank too much, a 'granny' in a psychogeriatric ward, a violent brother in Rampton and a grandfather suffering from 'senile decay'. Other examples included a suicide, a stroke victim and cases of claustrophobia and depression. Some respondents mentioned ways in which friends or relatives had been brought into contact with psychiatric services: Marilyn said that her sister was offered psychiatric help while her divorce was going through; Janet's daughter had a breakdown before taking her A-level examination and Brian Cleary talked about his father, who was always 'nervy' and how this had affected his mother, who eventually had a nervous breakdown.

Respondents were also asked whether they had been inside a psychiatric hospital prior to their own referral. Allowing that 'psychiatric hospital' was variously interpreted to mean not only mental illness hospitals but also those for the mentally handicapped and for geriatric patients, some one-third of them had gained some experience, in the capacity of visitor, employee or voluntary worker. For some the experience had been distressing, as in the case of Jane who had visited a psychiatric hospital some fifteen years previously while her mother was a patient and, more recently, to see a friend there. She found the hospital to be a frightening place and a depressing one. Following her own referral to a psychiatrist she felt stigmatised and thought that people would be 'frightened' of her. On the other hand, Eileen, who had also visited someone in a psychiatric hospital and had done voluntary work there (although she had not continued because, she said, the environment was 'off-putting' and 'scary') reported no stigma, no rejection, and no lack of sympathy from within her social circle when she herself needed psychiatric treatment.

There were, among the respondents, some who had never known anyone with a psychiatric problem and had never been inside a psychiatric hospital. One such was Ruth, who nevertheless felt stigmatised and thought that people would find her problems 'off-putting'.

Thus, many of the respondents had had some familiarity with the psychiatric setting and still more had known someone who had experienced psychiatric problems and treatment, prior to their own referral, even allowing that 'psychiatric' was sometimes applied to conditions that could not strictly be so defined. Even so, there was no discernible difference, with regard to the expectation and experience of stigma, between these respondents and the others who had no such knowledge.

TREATMENT SETTING

Does the extent of stigma experienced upon psychiatric referral vary, as between individuals, according to the place of treatment?

The recent trend has been to move from offering psychiatric treatment in large mental illness hospitals towards community-based services which include, among various forms of provision, the psychiatric departments of district general hospitals, out-patient clinics, day hospitals and assessment centres (DHSS, 1983; Trefgarne, 1984). One of the reasons for this trend is the somewhat hopeful assumption that treatment centred in the community will prove less stigmatising than treatment in traditional mental illness hospitals. There is little evidence to show whether or not this is so and the hope appears largely to derive from the notion that being a patient in a mental illness hospital is so stigmatising that any alternative would be better in this respect. Of course, there is plenty of evidence to demonstrate that stigma attaches to an inmate of a mental hospital (D'Arcy and Brockman, 1976; Meile and Whitt, 1981). Indeed, the stigma of mental illness is closely bound up with the stigma of the mental hospital, not surprisingly, as for past generations such hospitals provided the main (or only) setting for the treatment, detention and protection of disturbed patients. Indeed, so close was the connection between mental hospital and mental disturbance that researchers in the 1950s and 1960s found that admission to a mental hospital was the turning point at which a person was identified as 'mental' and stigmatised as such. The Cummings, in their influential work, observed that for lay groups 'mental illness is a condition which afflicts people who go to a mental institution' (Cumming and Cumming, 1957).

It is of interest to consider whether any features of these traditional mental institutions lend themselves to the stigmatising of their patients. Such places are usually located out of town, well away from main centres of population, their inmates thus 'put away' from the community of normals. Naming such an institution as the place of treatment can mean only that the problem is 'mental' since no other conditions are treated there. The buildings are more likely than not to be old, constructed in the last century, in a way that now appears off-putting, with long dismal corridors and separate wards (other types of older hospitals share these features). Perhaps, most importantly, these institutions are inevitably associated, in the minds of patients and visitors alike, with the past management of 'madness' and the emphasis on custody rather than treatment. The name of one such hospital, Bedlam, has passed into the language as a synonym for uncontrolled behaviour.

The mental hospital which respondents claimed previously to have visited or worked in, was generally just such an old, traditional one, located in a rural setting. By contrast, psychiatric treatment for the large majority of the respondents (seventy-five) was at the mental illness unit of the local general hospital; others met psychiatrists in the surgeries of their general practitioners and a few met them in their homes as well as in the mental illness unit.

The local general hospital is situated in a residential area of the city, the psychiatric unit being located in a newly-built wing, light, well-decorated and with spacious waiting areas. Nevertheless, those respondents who were treated there regarded it as stigmatising, and some related painful experiences:

> *Joanna:* 'I was waiting for my appointment in the lobby when a couple sat down next to me. The man said "I suppose you are waiting for visiting time like us". I did not say anything, so he went on: "I don't like visiting here, they are all loonies, and the worst is they look the same as us, so you don't know how bad they are. I reckon they should shut them away more". When he said this, I felt terrible, I felt so humiliated'.

John Curzon reported that on one occasion he went to the hospital by 'bus and met up with an acquaintance who was going to visit someone on a medical ward:

> 'When we got to the hospital, she asked which ward I wanted,

and when I said I was turning left she remarked "Oh you are visiting the loony ward, rather you than me". I felt angry but didn't say anything'.

Thus, the feelings discussed in this chapter are those of people who had never been treated in a traditional mental hospital, nor been in-patients of the psychiatric ward of a general hospital; they spoke as out-patients of the latter. It is impossible to say whether, had they been in-patients of either sort of institution, their stigma experience would have been any different. Only time will tell whether, once the worst features of the old-style mental hospitals have been relegated to history books, the mentally ill will still experience stigma despite more enlightened treatment.

TO CONCEAL OR TO DISCLOSE

It was said earlier that many respondents concealed their psychiatric referral from as many people as possible because they anticipated negative responses. Concealment is feasible since, unlike some other stigmatised conditions, psychiatric problems seldom constitute a visible stigma category; sufferers belong rather, in Goffman's words, to the category of potentially 'discreditable' people:

When his differentness is not immediately apparent, and is not known beforehand, when, in fact, he is a discreditable not a discredited person, then . . . the issue is not of managing tension generated during social contacts, but rather that of managing information about his failing. To display or not to display; to tell or not to tell; to let on or not to let on; to lie or not to lie; and in each case, to whom, how, when and where (Goffman, 1961, p. 42).

To conceal, or to disclose, seldom constituted a clear-cut choice; for most respondents the pattern was one of vacillation with responses being adapted to perceived attitudes. The choice had to be faced again and again, in each new situation, for each new human contact or renewal of an old one. A sympathetic attitude from someone would lead to further confidences, a hostile reception from another, bring about a reversion to concealment.

Studies of other stigma groups have likewise found this oscillating pattern of disclosure and withdrawal (Ablon, 1981). Members of these groups constantly find themselves evaluating the responses of others and devising strategies for future interaction in the light of such evaluations. To devise an unchanging strategy in the face of reactions which cannot be predicted is virtually impossible. Nor is it just a case of some people showing understanding and others not; according to several studies, responses of shame and rejection compete with feelings of sympathy and compassion (Doll *et al.,* 1976; Brockman *et al.,* 1979), resulting in frequent shifts in attitudes.

The workplace is, perhaps, the only area where a hard and fast decision needs to be made, since absence from duty invariably requires an explanation. Not all of the respondents had employment outside the home; many of the women were housewives and two of the men were unemployed. The majority had told their employers that they were having psychiatric treatment—many having been obliged to reveal this information since, as said, it was necessary to state the reason for being off work:

'It was going to this day hospital for two weeks and had to tell the boss'.

'I was at home for nearly two months, taking tablets and seeing the psychiatrist, I had to tell the supervisor'.

'He [the employer] wanted to check up whether I really went to a clinic, so I had to tell him which clinic it was'.

In most cases work colleagues were also aware of the treatment because, inevitably, the news tended to get around.

The attitudes of employers and colleagues alike were, for the most part, negative. Charles Kennedy, for example, who had to reveal details of his diagnosis and treatment, got no sympathy from his boss who remarked: 'Funny, a strapping big fellow like you being nervy, can't you pull yourself together'?

Frances, who suffered from spider phobia, had to tell her supervisor who thought it very funny but not a justification for being absent from work.

Not all experiences reflected negative evaluation. Kay, for

example, found her colleagues positive and supportive. She works in a large shop and when she told her colleagues:

> 'They were all nice about it. They quite understood that my husband's state had driven me to it (he was an alcoholic), and that I was trying to rise above things. They said that maybe the tablets will help and I must not worry about the work'

When it came to the question of whether or not to disclose to a prospective employer details of one's current or past psychiatric treatment, a changed situation was revealed, the consensus being that one should not volunteer information of that nature: 'out of the question'; 'that would be stupid'; 'I would never risk it', were typical comments. Uncertainty crept in when, in the course of elaborating their answers, respondents considered whether they would conceal the fact of their treatment if faced with a direct question (it was apparent that some of them had been confronted with application forms containing questions about health, emotional or psychiatric problems, and recent medical contacts). Many felt that they would avoid a direct lie, if only for fear of the consequences if the lie were discovered. Strategies for dealing with this problem were mapped out:

> 'Not on the application form, wouldn't stand a chance, I might tell at the interview'.

> 'It is not really relevant. I wouldn't say unless there was a question on the form. I would say it then'.

Anticipation of stigma from strangers, such as prospective employers, was strong, even in those who had met with favourable experiences from people within their individual social groups. It may well be that interviewers can seem hostile to job applicants, who might feel themselves to be in the vulnerable position of one who seeks something from another; moreover, the mere fact of being unemployed weakens the situation of the job applicant and heightens caution and anxiety. Some typical comments were:

> 'I would not tell, it is a stigma and with the job market in the

state it is, best not to say'.

'With all this unemployment, I wouldn't risk it, even if they found out later they may keep me on when they know I'm all right'.

Those respondents who felt that they had to tell prospective employers included two nurses who knew from experience that relevant questions would appear on application forms for nursing employment. There were also two sufferers from epilepsy, both of whom thought that by concealing this from an employer they would risk dismissal if they subsequently 'had a fit'; they applied this line of reasoning to their neurotic problems also. What is more, epilepsy appeared to them so stigmatising that any other condition might as well be admitted.

A few respondents said they would tell, in spite of anticipated stigma. Thus Stephen Caldwell remarked, somewhat belligerently: 'Yes, I would tell them, they must take me as I am. I've nothing to hide, I'm not "loopy"'. and Julie said: 'I am not ashamed, I would tell even if people take the wrong attitude'.

So, since psychiatric illness is 'invisible' (in the sense that deformity and some other stigmatised conditions are not) it can be concealed and the sufferer must decide. To some respondents this very invisibility seemed a drawback because without it they would not constantly face the need to rethink their strategy. Moreover, when concealment was decided upon the resultant anxiety over possible discovery seemed almost as bad as the anticipated stigma. Bridget said that she had to declare it to her colleagues and the supervisor because she could 'never have borne the strain'. Deborah explained that after the experience of being rejected by her neighbours, she decided never to tell anyone else, and found herself withdrawing from new contacts rather than forming friendships 'based on a lie' with the strain of discovery hanging over her. Another drawback of 'invisibilty' was the social embarrassment attendant upon sudden revelation: Ann told of a family gathering where she met an Australian cousin, Madge, for the first time. Madge was discussing her daughter's miscarriage when:

'My sister said "now you mustn't talk of upsetting things to her, she is neurotic, you know, and has to see a psychiatrist, we only talk about pleasant things with her". I can see Madge's face today; she froze and then forced a little smile and said "I mustn't go on chattering then. Anyway I must go and talk to the others"'.

When there are no visible indicators to give clues as to what to expect, surprise, shock and withdrawal may follow on awareness of the new, and unwelcome, information.

It is interesting to note that studies of other illness conditions have also reported that the very lack of 'visibility' can bring problems of social interaction as in the case of deaf people (Blaxter, 1976; Becker, 1981), and those with diabetes (Hopper, 1981), whereas the visibly disabled do not face the dilemma of concealment and the awkwardness of sudden discovery (Davis, 1964).

SOURCES OF STIGMA

We have seen that respondents were predisposed to expect stigma, but to what aspect of their predicament did they attribute this form of ostracisation? Was it the nature of their conditions or the psychiatric label attached to it? The answers may be important not just for the recipients of psychiatric treatment but also for those involved in the provision of services, for if it can be shown that the fact of psychiatric involvement is a significant contributor to stigma then it would be worth examining ways in which that involvement might be minimised or diguised (Crocetti *et al.*, 1974).

In considering this matter, a somewhat complex pattern emerged. For some respondents, their misfortune was all of a package: the problem, or more usually a cluster of problems, help-seeking from the family doctor, psychiatric referral and treatment, and stigma. These respondents could not view stigma as arising from any one aspect of their situation which, for them, constituted a single indivisible disaster.

Other respondents, however, felt able to separate the elements of the package and these could be divided into two categories. The smaller consisted of those whose initial problems had been defined by their respective social groups as evidently 'mental'. Often, in such cases, the condition had manifested itself in behaviour outside the accepted range, and disruptive of the customary pattern of social life. Other researchers of illness and disability have found that stigma is strong when the taken-for-granted world of daily interaction is threatened (Blaxter, 1976). To this category belonged Fiona, who had an obsession with cleanliness in the home. She explained that not only had she spent her waking hours cleaning her home, but when she visited her mother or her sister, she immediately 'set to and scrubbed out the cooker', and would break down and cry if they stopped her. Her relatives classed her as 'mental' and urged her to see a doctor. Liz said that she'd had a 'spectacular breakdown'. She jumped out of the window and neighbours saw her being taken away in an ambulance (to the General Hospital where she was treated for fractures and referred to a psychiatrist). Frances thought that her spider phobia which, among other things, had led to her screaming, running out of the house and demanding that her husband came home from work, had stigmatised her long before she saw a psychiatrist about her problem. She and the other respondents in this category had no difficulty in attributing stigma to the nature of their condition.

However, the larger group of those respondents who were able to consider the matter with some degree of objectivity felt that it was the psychiatric label attaching to the problem that stigmatised them: that once it became known that they had seen a psychiatrist, negative reaction followed. This feeling was exemplified by Colin Kinnison who very much wished that he had concealed his visits to the psychiatrist because his workmates 'never thought anything about my problem before but made much of it then'. The case of Ann, though, suggested that psychiatric labelling can be attached to treatment by a general practitioner, even when there is no subsequent referral to a psychiatrist. She said that it was her 'own doctor' who had told her that she was suffering from 'severe neurotic tension' which could lead to her becoming a real neurotic. When she repeated this to acquaintances at a Parent Teacher Association meeting, they 'whispered to one another and I felt I shouldn't have said it because it would be repeated to my daughter and I didn't want that'. Ann felt that her own doctor's diagnosis had stigmatised her.

All in all, it can be postulated that if psychiatric labelling can be avoided, and if problems can be handled by non-psychiatric services, for example, family practitioners, health visitors or even, where appropriate, self-help lay groups, then in some cases stigma may not arise or, at least, may be minimised. Those whose behaviour does not of itself invite lay labels of 'mental' and such-like would benefit most from the absence of professional psychiatric labelling.

By and large, recipients of psychiatric treatment feel stigmatised. There is an element of 'anticipatory socialisation' in their situation: they have been socialised into attaching stigma to people with 'mental' problems and thus expect it to be applied to themselves. Anticipation of stigma makes people reluctant to reveal their psychiatric problems to others and so to test responses. However, in this research, psychiatric diagnosis and treatment had invariably been communicated by respondents to at least some members of their social group and the interview material revealed many experiences of rejection and ridicule.

The constantly shifting nature of the problem needs to be stressed. A hostile response coming from someone from whom sympathy was expected leads to a reluctance to confide in others, while unexpected sympathy encourages confidences. Indeed, a criticism that can be levelled against Goffman's presentation of stigma is that he gives an impression of an unreal, static situation (Finkelstein, 1980).

There was a high degree of consensus among respondents regarding the desirability of concealing the fact of psychiatric treatment from prospective employers, and fear of unemployment appears to have made this situation worse. Widespread unemployment seems to have this unexpected by-product: it strengthens stigma. When competition for work is intense, job applicants hide their past psychiatric problems, thereby reaffirming the prejudice that a psychiatric condition is something to be ashamed of and to conceal.

Throughout the interviews, psychiatric problems were taken by respondents to embrace not only those severe disturbances which traditionally led to incarceration in mental hospitals but a range of conditions which could, loosely, be categorised as 'mental'. Alongside such terms as 'mental', 'senile', and 'nervy', respondents employed many colloquialisms denoting traditional attitudes of derogation and ridicule: loony, crazy, fruity, queer, nutty, loopy, were some of the terms used by respondents either to attribute sentiments to others, 'they think I am loopy'; or applied to themselves in order to deny their appropriateness, 'I am not crazy'. In a similar vein, mental illness hospitals were referred to as the 'loony house', 'funny farm', etc. It is interesting to note that this usage lingers on in popular parlance; that it is adhered to even by those who have every cause to eschew it and is applied by them even to mild psychiatric problems.

It was somewhat surprising to find that attending a general hospital's psychiatric clinic is felt to be stigmatising. This is a disappointment for many health professionals who hope for a substantial reduction of stigma when treatment is offered away from the traditional mental hospital. No doubt, long-established attitudes are slow to change; nevertheless, another possibility has to be faced, that anything regarded as 'mental' is so stigmatising that attitudes are likely to remain rigid and that other ways of avoiding stigma therefore need to be explored. It may well be that general practitioners who prefer not to refer their patients to psychiatrists, because of stigma, and who prefer not to describe patients' problems as 'psychiatric' for that reason, are right. Indeed, for the majority of respondents it was the psychiatric diagnosis and treatment rather than the neurosis itself that brought stigma upon them. It might, then, be thought preferable not to describe psychiatric problems as such and to arrange for consultation with psychiatrists to take place away from the psychiatric hospital setting, at home or in the general practitioner's surgery. But such subterfuge may serve only to enhance the feeling that mental illness is something to keep quiet about and hide.

5 Social Support

Individual suffering, whether it arises from mental or physical illness, places increased demands on the immediate social group. People move in social circles that may be extensive, limited or very narrow and within those circles relationships will range from the deep and abiding to the shallow and transitory. Social scientists have increasingly directed their attention to the 'quantity' and 'quality' of social relationships and to the correlation between these relationships and individual health. For example, it is argued that a high level of support will act as a buffer against the worst effects of stress, cushioning its impact on the individual concerned (Bloom, 1982; Waldron *et al.,* 1982). There have been studies of the ways that social support levels may influence both the aetiology of diseases and their progression, the latter being of particular importance to people having to cope with long-term and debilitating conditions. Indeed there is evidence that adequate social support can improve adjustment, reduce the risk of complications and speed recovery (Venters, 1981; Funch and Mettlin, 1982).

The causal connection between neurotic disorders and the lack of social bonds has been discussed in Chaper 1. Writing about the influence of social support on the course of such disorders, Klerman (1978), found that supportive relationships tend to deteriorate as depression continues, reinforcing patients' feelings of worthlessness and adversely affecting the course of the illness. Others, too, have commented on the harmful influence that a poor quality of support exerts upon symptoms, which are maintained instead of improving (Weissman and Paykel, 1974; Vaughn and Leff, 1976).

Social support is a somewhat inadequately understood concept and it is not easy to establish what constitutes strong or weak support (Pilisuk and Froland, 1978). All men and women have social relationships, being social creatures, but the term 'social support' suggests something other than the generalised interdependence of all members of society. It has both an emotional and a practical content, emotional in the provision of sympathy and affection, creating in its object the assurance of being loved and a sense of belonging; practical in the provision of assistance, financial, physical or whatever. Emotional support may come from just one individual or from many, and may be of varying intensity; practical support may likewise derive from one source or several and can be provided cheerfully and willingly or with reluctance. In such manner, the quantity and quality of support accorded to each individual will differ, to some degree, from that accorded to another.

Without social support people are liable to feel lonely, isolated, even unwanted, and a growing body of research literature has drawn attention to the quantitative lack of contacts suffered by many housewives, particularly those having no outside employment. Mothers of young children, in Sue Sharpe's (1984) study, spoke repeatedly of their lack of adult conversation and of spending many hours alone, or with only young children for company. The respondents of Ann Oakley's (1974) study of housework and the working-class housewives studied by Dorothy Hobson (1978), voiced similar sentiments; they felt cut off from the companionship and interests of others. Such women experience a sense of 'captivity' at home, a feeling of being 'trapped' (Gavron, 1966). For some, this quantitative lack of contacts is accompanied by a qualitative lack also, as when there is no friend or relative, even at a distance, with whom personal matters can occasionally be discussed. The findings of Brown and Harris (1978) demonstrate the link between depression in women and the poverty of their supportive relationships.

Housewives are by no means the only people vulnerable in this way. Studies of the elderly living alone (Jerrome, 1981; Evers, 1985), the physically disabled (Blaxter, 1976), women looking after handicapped children and adults (Voysey, 1975) and new immigrants (Lynam, 1985), have reported many instances of such people spending long hours alone, lacking integration, and consequently feeling isolated and cut off. Even when there is adequate support in the quantitative sense, it may still lack qualities of intimacy and companionability. For example, elderly people living with their children and grandchildren may nevertheless feel the want of others of their own age group, with whom they can discuss the happenings of past years.

In the following sections the social support received by the women respondents of the sample will be examined and compared with the corresponding experience of the men.

ISOLATION RELIEVED BY CASUAL SOCIAL CONTACTS

Housewives who have no outside employment are likely to be alone for much of the day, allowing that a degree of isolation is inherent in housework, done as it is in the privacy of the home. Spending many hours of the day alone, or with only young children for company, was the experience of a number of women who, in their own words, felt trapped, cut off or abandoned.

Sarah, 37, two children 6 months and 3½ years: 'I'm alone too much, on some days I am on my own all day and all evening as well. My husband goes to work at eight in the morning and comes home at four, but goes back to do overtime at seven. We hardly see him. I have no friends. It will be better in the summer when we can go out . . . these long hours alone in the winter, I am trapped in the house'.

Of all these housewives, the loneliest were those who were childless or whose grown-up offspring had left home: they lacked even the casual contacts enjoyed among young mothers taking their children to school or the recreation ground. By the very nature of their problems, neurotic women are inhibited from seeking companionship, victims of the kind of vicious circle noted previously, isolation tending to neurosis which in turn limits still further social activity. Dread of being overtaken by an attack of panic, fear of picking up germs, and obsession with housework (the two latter often related) were problems that reinforced isolation.

All in all, the women whose work was entirely in their own homes had fewer casual contacts than had the women with outside employment, much depending on the nature thereof. Perhaps the most isolated woman was Shelagh, who had part-time work as a home-help, four mornings per week. She would walk across the park to her place of employment, let herself into an empty house, complete her cleaning tasks and return home, without having spoken a word to anyone. She would go to buy cigarettes or ask someone the time 'just to hear the sound of my own voice'. Shelagh was unlucky in that she had no relatives living close by and her husband was often away from home. She felt desperately lonely. Others worked in situations that were hardly less isolated: one, a restaurant worker, spent the hours of her employment alone in the kitchen; another, a nurse, worked the night shift in an old folks' home, passing many a night without speaking to anyone. These cases illustrate that having employment does not necessarily provide a shield against loneliness.

It is for just such isolated people that casual contacts can have an important meaning. Research has shown that people newly moved into an area can feel themselves surrounded by strangers, seemingly indifferent if not unfriendly; later, as they come to know the neighbours, the postman and the tradespeople, these feelings give way to a sense of belonging. For lonely people, the most casual of contacts can assume an importance beyond its intrinsic worth; a 'good morning!', a wave of the hand, a few words exchanged with the milkman, can help to relieve the emptiness of the day and lessen the sense of being cut off from the everyday life of the community. Brief conversations in front of the school with other mothers, chats over the fence with neighbours and so on, the mere minutiae of social intercourse, can have a special value to those affected by loneliness.

Shelagh was untypical, however. Most of the women had what they regarded as an adequate number of casual contacts of the sort which provided them with the opportunity to exchange a few words. Casual contacts seldom provide social support in any meaningful sense of the term although, unexpectedly, some women received offers of help from quite casual acquaintances in time of crisis. Jill, whose younger child was deaf, was pleasantly surprised by an offer from another young mother to take the child to playschool: 'I've only met her once or twice before but she said she'd heard I'd had a breakdown and wanted to help'.

It is noteworthy that psychiatric illness and treatment were topics on which conversation with casual accquaintances was not possible. On health-related topics in general, discussions with casual acquaintances are conducted in the waiting rooms of doctors' surgeries and in shops where medicines are bought, among other places. The women of the survey found that while they could join in casual conversation on many such issues (for example, children's health), they could not venture upon their neurotic problems, for fear of rebuff.

EMOTIONAL SUPPORT: EXPECTATIONS AND REALITY

Casual contacts are of importance to the very lonely. Most married women do not live in conditions of extreme physical isolation, there are people around them with whom ties can be formed. In contemporary society generally, members of a person's family, kin group, friends, neighbours and work associates are potential sources of support and this group of people constitutes the individual's primary social network.

It will be remembered that in Chapter 1, in the section headed The Social Causation Approach, reference was made to Scott Henderson's postulation of an association between the mental health of individuals and the extent of their success in forming social relationships; also cited was George Brown's research finding that persons who enjoyed close confiding relationships were less vulnerable to depression than those who lacked such supportive relationships. In their study of depression in women Brown and Harris (1978) wrote:

We have found that if a woman does not have an intimate tie, someone she can trust and confide in, particularly a husband or boyfriend, she is much more likely to break down in the presence of a severe event or major difficulty (p. 278).

During the interviews, the women respondents of the present research project were asked to name the person (or persons) in their lives in whom they could readily confide, who was interested in their problems and to whom they could turn for support.

Table 5.1: Persons to whom women turned for emotional support

Husband	24
Female friend	10
Sister, sister-in-law, cousin	13
Mother	3
Mother-in-law, older female relative	3
Grown-up children	2
Father, brother	2
No one	8
Total	65

HUSBANDS AS SOURCES OF EMOTIONAL SUPPORT

For married people, spouses occupy a special position as potential providers of emotional support, not only because of their physical proximity but because, according to Western cultural expectation, spouses share in each other's lives.

However, studies of marital relationships have found that this is not necessarily the case, especially for women. Elizabeth Bott, in her influential early work on network structure and conjugal roles, showed that many wives relied for emotional and practical support not on their husbands but on female relatives and friends (1957). In certain types of social networks, husband and wife tended to have separate circles of friends of the same sex, and more support was derived from these external relationships than from spouses. Myra Komarovsky (1967), in a study of American working-class families, described the marriages as having little 'psychological intimacy' and little expectation of companionship. The couples felt that intimate friendship and emotional support were for persons of the same sex.

Komarovsky suggested that in times of emotional stress, especially in the case of women, relationships outside marriage were likely to be called upon for support and that in such cases heavy demands were made on the network of female kin and friends.

More recent studies, such as Sarsby's (1972) on British teenagers, Rubin's (1976), on working-class family life and Sharpe's (1984) on working mothers in Britain, indicate that Komarovsky's contention still applies; emotional support and intimacy in marriage is no more usual than is failure to achieve it. Other research has shown that practical help, too, may not be forthcoming from husbands (Oakley, 1974).

It is noteworthy that out of the sixty-five women in the study, only twenty-four named husbands as their main confidants and supporters; even this comparatively low level of apparent conjugal concord was belied by the research finding that almost without exception these women regarded their marriages as unsatisfactory.

So the majority of the women did not regard their husbands as their main confidants. Nevertheless, most of them made efforts to gain their husbands' support in time of need. For example, when they felt 'especially low' or 'panicky' or when they tried to decide whether or not to go to the psychiatrist, they first attempted to talk to their husbands. They reported failure.

Nor were all the twenty-four women whose husbands constituted their main support satisfied with their situation: some were unhappy and wished it otherwise. They turned to their husbands because there was no one else.

Feminist writers have noted a particular contradiction in the situation of certain married women: while it is the husband who stands in the way of the woman's attainment of a satisfactory life, he is also the proximate, sometimes, indeed the only, person available as a potential provider of support, and the wife is obliged to turn to him.

Iris, 24, no children: 'There is only my husband. I wish there was someone else. Mostly, I keep my thoughts to myself. I hoard my thoughts, then I get upset and tell my husband because there is nobody else. I usually regret it afterwards. He is part of the trouble, but who else can I talk to'?

Bridget, 29, two children 4 and 7: 'I wish I had more people, I wish I had a woman friend, My husband is there but he doesn't want to talk, not like women talk to each other. He doesn't understand. He just says, don't bother me with nonsense'.

For Iris, Bridget and others, marital conflict was part of life and contributed to neurosis. There is certainly some irony in the situation, where the only person they could turn to for emotional support in a crisis was the one with whom they were in conflict.

Conflict was not the only marital situation which prevented wives from obtaining their husbands' support. Some husbands were critical or hostile and this will be discussed later but, more often, they were simply uninterested or unavailable: they were not at home, or were busy with other things, or just not willing to pay attention to their wives' problems. 'I can't talk to my husband, he wouldn't listen' and similar expressions of marital indifference were frequently uttered during the interviews both by women who said that support was not forthcoming from their husbands and by those who named their husbands as sources of support in the absence of anyone else.

Clearly, marriages characterised by the withdrawal of husbands from the partnership were not settings in which confidences could be exchanged. It was the experience of several women that their husbands had their own concerns, their own lives to lead and were inaccessible to their wives' emotional needs; some husbands managed not to notice or to ignore even the serious problems of their wives which affected domestic life and childcare.

In a classic early study of marital situations characterised by a climate of alienation and withdrawal which led to wives' admission to a mental hospital, Sampson and his colleagues described a typical couple thus:

For two years before hospitalisation Mrs Rand was troubled by various somatic complaints, persistent tension, difficulty in sleeping, a vague but disturbing conviction that she was a sinner and an intermittent state of acute panic. Mr Rand was minimally aware of her distress. He worked up to fourteen hours a day, including weekends, in his store and eventually a second job took him out of home three evenings a week. On those infrequent occasions when his wife's worries forced themselves on his attention, he dismissed them curtly as absurd and turned once again to his own affairs. (Sampson *et al.*, 1968, p. 206).

In the present research similar situations were described:

> *Amy, 48, three children 8, 17 and 22:* 'I tried to tell him about my panic attacks but he didn't listen. He is always too busy with his carpentry when he is at home, there is no opportunity to tell him anything. Last winter I had such bad times that my doctor tried to talk to him but he didn't want to know; he says "I provide for you, you don't need anything, you don't have to work, you still moan, what else can I do"? All he asks for is not to be bothered'.

Men's failure to appreciate their wives' emotional needs, and their unwillingness or inability to provide emotional support, are likely to be rooted in Western cultural values. They would not discuss such matters in pub or club, that would be 'women's talk'; so, also would they associate expressions of care and affection with the feminine gender role.

There were women who described their husbands as 'loving' or 'very understanding', but these were only a minority.

FRIENDS AND RELATIVES AS SOURCES OF SUPPORT

As Table 5.1 shows, twenty-three women considered a female friend or relative as the person in whom they could best confide. These friends and relatives were mainly of the same generation as the women respondents whose intimates they were.

These twenty-three women enjoyed a support system somewhat similar to the close-knit type of network described by Elizabeth Bott (1957). According to Bott, such a network is characterised by cohesiveness and is of a localised nature; it will contain people who are likely to have lived in the same neighbourhood for most of their lives, working locally in similar employment, and all knowing each other well. It contrasts with the loose-knit network characterised by residentially mobile people whose relatives and friends are likely to be scattered. It is in close-knit networks that support is typically obtained from others of the same sex. However, unlike some women with this kind of support system, who turn first to their mothers, (Young and Wilmott, 1962) this group of women in the sample turned rather to women of approximately their own age; friends, sisters and sisters-in-law were their main source of support. Again, unlike the usual situation in close-knit networks where support is likely to come from a number of sources, among these particular women there were very few who could name more than two intimates, some only one. Thus, quantitatively, support was poor but on the other hand this part of the sample had the most stable and satisfactory relationship with providers of support. They could talk frankly to chosen network members who, in turn, were interested and willing to exchange confidences.

The number of women who obtained their main support from people of a different generation was comparatively few, such support deriving mainly from mothers and older relatives or from adult children.

How did the friends and relatives who were nominated as main sources of support come to be so regarded? What factors governed the choice of confidants? As discussed earlier, choice, for some women, was restricted to the one or two persons available, although generally the nature of the confidence that women wanted to share influenced the choice of intimates.

The subjects about which the women most felt the need of close and confiding discussion could broadly be divided into two categories. First, all those matters relating to marriage, children, biological processes, domestic duties, relationships with in-laws, loneliness, etc., which on one level can form the topics of conversation at coffee-mornings and on similar occasions when women meet together, but which can be discussed in depth only with an intimate female friend or relative. Second, their neurotic illness and psychiatric treatment was a subject that the women could only discuss with someone from whom sympathy and understanding could be expected; people with whom they could discuss almost anything else might shy away from mental illness. However, to divide the subjects that the women most wanted to discuss into two categories is not to suggest that they could necessarily make such a distinction: matters which normally would form the common currency of social intercourse fell into a sort of 'grey area' when they were perceived as bearing on neurotic problems.

With regard to the first group of subjects, the women could

discuss some matters with their husbands and most of them had some women friend or relative available for 'women's chat', but, confronted by a 'sea of troubles' the women needed as intimates others who had experienced problems of a similar magnitude, from whom sympathy and understanding might be expected, and thus they gravitated towards network members who themselves had been through chronic illness, divorce, bereavement and other kinds of adversity, such people being preferred, as confidants, to those who were apparently trouble-free and happy.

It was much more difficult to find intimates with whom the neurotic illness itself could be discussed. Many women would have liked to find someone within their network with whom they could share the experience of depression, anxiety or phobia, or someone who had had psychiatric treatment, and so would be in a position to provide understanding and support, but few were able to locate such a person. Most of them had tried, with one or more persons, to discuss their feelings and experiences, but had failed to make themselves understood. There was complete agreement on two points: first, that people with personal experience of neurotic problems came nearest to understanding and, if available, were the best choices for confidences and support; second, that it was not possible for one person entirely to understand the personal experiences, innermost feelings and sufferings of another, and that it was futile to expect total empathy.

Yvonne, 35: 'No one can understand agoraphobia who hasn't experienced it. My Mum tried and my brothers tried but they can't, and I can't explain to them . . . even if you do experience it you can't really understand somebody else, it's different for different people . . . it depends on what sparks it off, for one thing'.

Joyce, 29: 'You can talk to some people about depression. I can talk to my sister and my friend. My sister had depression when she was a teenager and my friend had post-natal depression. But nobody can really understand what you are feeling. I can say that confidently. It is an incredible thing, hard to explain even to doctors'.

Jill, 22: 'Nobody can entirely understand, not completely, you can't understand it yourself. Nobody else knows what is running through your mind and you can't explain. To give you an example, I can get so jealous, the psychiatrist says it's an obsession. I would be ashamed to tell anybody what my thoughts are . . .. Maybe somebody who'd been through depression like mine would understand it a little, but not entirely'.

In spite of failures to make people understand, and the conviction that total empathy is unattainable, many women persevered with discussions and confidences, hoping for support and reassurance, and in this, quite a number of them succeeded.

Researchers studying sufferers from diverse diseases and disabilities find that such people expect, and may quite often receive, understanding and support from those with the experience of similar problems. Indeed, this is one way of utilising the relevant experience of the social group. The exchange of information that takes place within a social group indicates to the members of that group the 'right' ways of thinking and acting according to its established norms. Health-related discussions indicate to individuals the socially approved ways of behaving in illness situations. The experience of depression, anxiety or phobia is an intensely personal one and when people try to understand and attach meaning to that experience they have recourse to the explanations and meanings provided by their group culture (Miles, 1978).

Those women who were able to discuss their condition and treatment with an intimate friend or relative who had some relevant experience, found reassurance; they were not alone in their distress and sharing the experience provided support. They were reassured as to the propriety of their behaviour, for example in continuing with psychiatric treatment; the social approval thus gained was specially valuable to those whose husbands disapproved of the treatment.

Joanne, 46: 'It was a comfort to know someone who had experienced it. I was desperately upset at first, I thought nobody can be in such a state who is not mad . . . I thought I was going mad, I was frightened. It was such a relief to tell all about it to Meg, she had panic attacks herself. She went to a psychologist and he really helped her, so I thought I am doing the right thing . . . when I get too panicky now I ring Meg and she says "I know how you are feeling", it's odd what a difference it makes'.

LACK OF CLOSE TIES

There were eight women who had no confidants, no one they could talk to about their intimate thoughts and feelings. They were some of the most lonely and unhappy people in the study, the others being women who attempted to confide in their husbands but met with coolness or hostility. It was for these women that 'weak ties' with casual contacts had the greatest value.

Of course, people differ in their desire to confide in others and differ also in their expectations as to the quantity and quality of support to be expected from those nearest to them. Feelings of loneliness and of not belonging, and the adequacy or otherwise of support, have to be viewed within the framework of personal wishes and expectations.

Moreover, the cultural valuations placed on intimacy and sharing as against those values placed on reserve and independence, vary between different social groups within the wider society. There was certainly a minority of women who insisted that they had no wish to confide in anyone, but preferred to keep their troubles to themselves. However, the majority wished for intimate bonds and emotional support.

Quite usual was the situation of women who were caught in a double-bind situation; on one hand they were told by psychiatrists to talk frankly to intimates, not to 'bottle up' their feelings and to 'open up' marital conflicts; on the other, they had no one with whom they could conduct such discussions but their unwilling husbands or relatives.

FEAR OF BEING A BURDEN

Perhaps the most striking feature of the women's search for

emotional support was their fear of placing too many demands on their close friends and relatives. A constant dread of overstraining social network ties characterised the relationships of most women. 'I don't want to be a burden' was repeated again and again.

Diane, 34: 'You can't pester people with your troubles, even if they are family. I can talk to Frances [sister-in-law] she is easy to talk to and she understands a lot. She has children the same age and she had her share of troubles. But I don't want to run to her too much . . . I have times when I am so depressed, for a week or more, that I need somebody every day, just to be here and keep me company, but I don't ask her . . . I daren't ask too much'.

Patricia, 29: 'My friend is very understanding, she helps in many ways, just by being with me. Some days that is the biggest help. There are days when I am alone and I get desperate and I think I'll call her, but I don't do it. I don't want to be a burden. There is nobody else I can really talk to, I wish there was. I was very close to my sister before she married, but she is too far now'.

There were several reasons for this fear of becoming a burden. The very consciousness that the need for companionship and emotional support is so great, in fact potentially unlimited, lends weight to feelings of being burdensome, especially when the number of intimates comprises only one or two persons. Rejection is not risked. Both Diane and Patricia felt that there were times when they needed their understanding friend to be there constantly, even though they realised that such a demand would be impossible to fulfil. Joanna, who telephoned her friend in times of troubles and was reassured by her, added, 'I don't do it too often, I don't want to be a nuisance'. Efforts were made by the women to reduce demands on their few intimates to what was perceived as 'not too much', but the fear of overstraining people's patience and goodwill persisted.

Other groups in society whose need for help and support is very great, feel reluctant to place what may be seen as exorbitant demands on their network. In the case of the chronically sick and the physically disabled Blaxter (1976) found some patients concerned not to 'run out of credit' and 'accumulate too large a debt' (p. 57). The actual experience of rejection by some relatives and friends was another reason for respondents' fear of making too many demands.

> *Kim, 28:* 'I don't want to impose on people. I don't like to ask, I am always afraid that they don't want to know. After I'd taken an overdose, I lost some friends. They don't want to know you when you are down'.

Others, too, had the experience of losing contact with people who, before the neurosis became troublesome, were thought to be close friends. This is a by no means unusual feature of social networks in contemporary urban society: quite often people appear to withdraw in a crisis, just when additional support is needed. Thus, for example, patients suffering from multiple sclerosis complain that they lose their friends (Miles, 1979), couples find that after their marriage breaks down their contacts with friends and relatives decline (Hart, 1976; Evason, 1980), unemployment and chronic illness weaken bonds with family and friends (Blaxter, 1976; McKee, 1983).

Quantitative paucity of support was another reason why those women who had only one or two intimates hesitated to put those relationships too much to the test. Moreover, their low self-esteem caused them to question their ability to reciprocate emotional support. They could not believe themselves to be of equal value to their intimates.

Thus there was a general expectation that even the most intimate relationship could be pushed too far. That, taken in conjunction with a quantitative lack of support, meant that for many of the women isolation was an ever-present threat.

Some women endeavoured to lessen their demands on others by not seeking practical help from the same person or persons to whom they turned for emotional support. This feature of 'not being a burden' was characteristic of women whose potential source of assistance was restricted to only one or two individuals.

THE REVERSE OF SUPPORT: CRITICISM AND DISAPPROVAL FROM CLOSE RELATIONS

Friends, neighbours and more distant relatives may or may not provide emotional support; those who do not want to be involved can just drop the relationship. For husbands, mothers and close relatives there is another alternative, which is to continue in familial roles while expressing criticism and disapproval. Husbands, perhaps, play the most important role because, if they take this line, their disapproval and failure to lend support will constantly be felt. Psychiatric problems and treatment can hardly be hidden from husbands as they can be, albeit with difficulty, from parents and other relatives.

Several women had husbands and mothers who lacked belief in the reality of their problem and disapproved of their psychiatric treatment; some other near relations (sisters and brothers) adopted similar attitudes. A frequently expressed view was that the woman was making too much of her troubles; that she was inclined to 'give in', that she did not 'make enough effort' to overcome difficulties. Women were admonished to 'snap out of it' or 'pull yourself together'. Some husbands were contemptuous of 'women's troubles' and said they were due to the women having 'too much time to think' about problems and having 'too easy a life'.

Another focus of disapproval was the psychiatric treatment: doctors' diagnoses were pronounced to be 'nonsense' and treatment regarded as 'unnecessary' and 'making things worse'. Discussions with psychiatrists were viewed with suspicion and apprehension.

Ida, 52: 'My husband doesn't like my seeing a psychiatrist. He thinks I make too much of my moods and brood on things too much . . . . He doesn't even try to understand . . .'

Becky, 21: 'Kevin is very unsympathetic. He thinks I should snap out of it and not complain. He says "I am sick of your moans . . .". He is sarcastic about the psychiatrists. He says "I don't want a nutcase for a wife". It undermines my confidence'.

The situation of the wife, husband or near relative of someone who has been diagnosed as neurotic is a complex one. A common response to serious illness is an attempt to normalise or, at least, to minimise it, especially if the condition is potentially life-threatening, stigmatising or fearful in some other way. When a woman is referred to a psychiatrist, the perceived threat is of the much feared and stigmatising mental illness: the response of husbands and mothers is likely to be to play it down in the hope that the diagnosis will prove to be mistaken or the illness insignificant. A husband may feel responsible for his wife's troubles, an unpleasant feeling to be pushed away rather than acknowledged. Inability to keep one's wife happy and contented can be regarded as a slur on one's manliness, a failure to perform a husband's role. Moreover, psychiatrists often direct attention to marital relationships and this in itself can put husbands on the defensive.

> *Alice, 33:* 'He doesn't like me going to the psychiatrist. He says the psychiatrist can't do anything, I have to do it myself and maybe he is right in this . . . I think he just hates the idea that I am nuts and doesn't want to face it that I have problems. Deep down, he is probably afraid that he caused it and that he wasn't a good husband to me . . . I think the psychiatrist may help me, I want to give it a chance. I don't mention it much at home, try to keep it to myself now, . . . not a secret exactly but play it down'.

Several women mentioned that their husbands felt themselves criticised by psychiatrists; after a session they asked 'what did he say about me?' The thought of their wives repeating marital secrets and intimate details is also distasteful to many husbands, who would ask afterwards 'what did you tell him?' Some mothers felt similarly upset by their daughters' psychiatric sessions and asked of them what was said about parental relationships and childhood events. Interestingly, even some otherwise understanding and supportive husbands were critical of psychiatric treatment. The strongly-held cultural expectation that the family is a self-contained and happy unit providing for its members' security and contentment, means that people expect the family to cope; calling in an outside expert to help with what can be regarded as a family problem indicates a failure to cope. It shatters the image of the well managed, cohesive and competent family.

Whatever the reason for criticism and disapproval, lack of support by husbands, mothers and other close relatives is painful because there is a strong cultural expectation that the immediate family can be relied upon. The 'happy family' is an ideal of contemporary society; indeed, Oakley argues that it is the 'major paradigm of social relations in which the inhabitants of modern technologically complex societies are encouraged to believe' (Oakley, 1981B, p. 242). People are brought up to expect love, assistance and support from marital and parental relationships; when cultural expectations clash with reality, they tend to think in terms of individual causes; they assume that something has gone wrong with their particular relationships while continuing to believe unquestioningly in the myth of the happy family. Problems are located in individuals (unfeeling husband, irritable wife, unnatural mother) blame is imputed and individual solutions sought. Many of the women's psychiatrists encouraged them to look for such causes.

Women struggling with neurotic problems and not finding the support they expected from their husbands or mothers have the added burden of regarding this state of affairs as unnatural and probably brought about by themselves.

Where the mothers were critical or disapproving, the surprise and hurt appeared even greater than in cases where the husbands behaved in this way. Women, traditionally, are providers of love, affection and emotional support and there was a strong expectation that mothers would fulfil this function. For example, Frances, whose breakdown was attributed by herself, and by the psychiatrists, to her struggles with her alcoholic husband, said 'What hurts me so much is that my mother is unsympathetic. She must be a very strange mother, other women get a lot of help from their Mums, but mine doesn't care'.

PROBLEMS OF THE SICK ROLE

Even before tackling the difficulties discussed so far in this chapter, the women had to confront the issue of whether neurosis is an illness at all; like people generally they were undecided.

Much has been written on the sick role in recent years: the privileges attached to it (exemption from normal role duties for its duration and exemption from blame for the condition) and the obligations on which the privileges rest (the wish to get well and co-operation with efforts to achieve this end) (Parsons, 1951; Zola, 1973; Gallagher, 1976). Usually, the sick role has to be claimed by the individual concerned and the claim has to be accepted as legitimate by the immediate social group, for the sick person to be able to abandon ordinary social obligations without the imputation of blame. Both sufferer and social group have to concede that the sickness is genuine, and that it is severe enough to merit appropriate changes in the allocation of duties and in social relationships. Sufferers from neurotic problems themselves find it difficult to decide whether or not their problem is an 'illness'; in this study hardly any of the women so referred to their condition (see Chapter 2) even though most of the psychiatrists and some of the physicians had informed their patients that they were suffering from a medical condition. There is no consensus among health professionals as to whether depression, agoraphobia and anxiety should be called medical conditions at all, and as a result contradictory messages reach the sufferers, creating in them more doubts and uncertainties. The cultural expectation, shared by the women in the study, is that a genuinely sick person is physically unwell and unable to work, but unlike this stereotype, the women felt physically quite well most of the time and their complaints of breathlessness, sweating, sleeplessness etc., were intermittent and minor enough to be accommodated within the lay definition of adequate health. In not claiming to be sick these women conformed to the pattern of women in general, who, from evidence, are often reluctant to claim the sick role because of the pressure of domestic duties and because they think of themselves as 'carers' rather than the cared for.

Many husbands were even more reluctant to regard their wives' neurotic problems as illness, and accord them the sick role, than were the women themselves. Their wives appeared physically healthy to these men and did not fit their image of a sick person. Thus the sick role was neither claimed nor accorded within such families.

Of course, there are many minor ailments among the population for which the sick role is not adopted and normal social activities not seriously interrupted. On the other hand there are chronic ailments, requiring long-term treatment (such as heart conditions) and permanent disabilities (for example, the loss of a limb) where the social roles of sufferers could be said to be ambiguous in that they are not sick enough to be obliged to abandon their social obligations nor as robust as others to carry them out. Furthermore, the social arrangements which need to be made to help such individuals must be expected to continue for a long time or indefinitely. In such cases a modified sick role may be assumed, in which the individuals concerned have to limit but not give up entirely the performance of their normal social activities. Usually, this limitation of role performance is accepted by the social group on condition that the sufferers limit their demands to the minimum necessary and do not expect too many concessions (Freidson, 1970).

Sufferers from neurosis, when their condition is accepted as an illness, are in the same ambiguous position as the chronically sick and impaired; they are able to carry out normal social roles but their performance is limited. What constitutes adequate role performance in such circumstances is always uncertain, and disputes go on within families as to the legitimacy of the demands made by the neurotic. For example some women struggling with depression complained of always being tired, even exhausted, and of not being able to face getting up in the morning. Such complaints are often taken as signs of laziness by the social group.

Sally, 28: 'I used to become exhausted very quickly and quite a few relatives insinuated that I was lazy for sitting down a lot. They didn't know I was depressed and it was no good telling them'.

The fact that the doctors who diagnosed and treated the problems as 'illness' were psychiatrists tended to increase both uncertainties and disapproval. Laymen are dubious about psychiatry, and stigma attaches to the whole psychiatric enterprise. As legitimisers of illness, psychiatrists are in a far from clear position and their verdicts are more likely to be disputed than are those of physicians.

Research has shown men to be more out of sympathy with a psychiatric interpretation of problems and less likely to seek psychiatric help than are women. Certainly, many of the husbands appeared to their wives to be less inclined to accept the views and validations of psychiatrists than they were themselves.

PRACTICAL HELP AND ASSISTANCE

How much practical help is expected, and forthcoming, from relatives, friends and neighbours? Potential support is not necessarily translated into effective support and although this may be more true of the loose-knit networks, where distance, time and cost of travel may be among the inhibiting factors, it is true also of close-knit networks, where sickness, other responsibilities and troubles of their own may limit the help that members are able to provide at any given time.

In this survey, the most urgent need for practical assistance centred around children and domestic work; need for financial and other assistance was rare. Many women needed practical assistance of the kind that neighbours and the wider kin group routinely provide, but which they found difficult to obtain. For example, several agoraphobics needed help with taking children to school, and companions for shopping expeditions or routine visits to dentists, hairdressers etc. Those who had intermittent bouts of depression also needed, at those times, help with the shopping, cooking and looking after young children; some whose condition caused them to be 'disorganised' needed to borrow household things that they had run out of. These are small favours, usually fairly easy to obtain, but special difficulties arose to block customary channels of assistance. The two main difficulties were lack of reciprocity and the indefinite duration of the need.

Women in general find little difficulty in seeking favours on a reciprocal basis: for instance, taking turns in accompanying children to school. But an agoraphobic, to cite one example, cannot enter into an 'exchange' scheme of this sort;

moreover, a neighbour who agreed to take the children of an agoraphobic mother to school, or shop for her, would have to continue that service indefinitely. The essence of the re-allocation of tasks, following the assumption of the sick role, lies in the temporary nature of the arrangement. In acute illness the probable duration can be estimated, however inaccurately, but for the social group of the agoraphobic or depressed woman no such estimate is possible; indeed the fear is that the condition will be long-term. Furthermore, the help given to someone in acute illness is regarded as potentially reciprocal, but such an assumption cannot be made for those suffering from neurosis.

Yvonne (again): 'My neighbour took the children to school for a time and my mother-in-law helped with the shopping. But I can't ask them to go on doing things for me, they soon get fed up . . .. Luckily the children are old enough to go to school on their own, but I don't know what to do about Kerry [youngest of three children, aged 2] she will have to go to play school soon. Maybe another neighbour . . . I don't like to ask because there is nothing I can do in return'.

Sally (again): 'A lot of people helped after Terry was born and I had post-natal depression. My cousin came down from the North, and others too . . .. But when the depression went on, they stopped. People are kind at first but they expect you to recover very quickly, and lose patience. You need just to let time pass. Even my Mum thought I was lazy and a hypochondriac, she said it was time I pulled myself together. You can't ask people to help you all the time, they get tired of you, and don't want to know . . .'.

Marion 33: 'I remember the neighbourhood school scheme. When I first had the panic attacks, my two children were taken to school by three or four neighbours, in turn. It was fine for a time, then they saw I wasn't getting better and wanted to pull out. When the school started again in September, nobody offered, and when I asked they said they had stopped the scheme. I know it isn't true, they just dropped me because I can't take their children'.

There were other constraints on the provision of support. Some couples had moved house prior to the onset of the neurotic condition, a fact which may, in any case, have contributed to that condition.

Both Bott and Komarovsky pointed out that when husband and wife rely on friends and relatives, rather than each other, for support, the disruption of network arrangements consequent upon moving to another neighbourhood can have very damaging effects. Having lost their previous support system, the spouses are thrown back on each other and the resultant increased demands put a strain on the marriage. In this survey it was found that most of the women who had no intimate relationships with anyone, together with some of those who relied exclusively on their husbands for support, had moved house within a few years previously and had not succeeded in integrating into a new network to replace the old. By contrast very few of the women who enjoyed close ties with female relatives and friends had recently moved.

Those who had moved were quite clear about the adverse effects of living in a new neighbourhood.

Iris, 24: 'I was miserable when we moved to the city. My husband was all right, he had his work, he had his new mates, but I didn't. I couldn't get work here and it got me down, being at home alone . . . I had friends before, some I knew from school, and there was my sister; I've lost them now, they are too far'.

Bridget, 29: 'I lost all my friends when we came to this home. The house is much better, we have a garden and the children are happier. We were on the fifth floor before. But I paid a high price, I lost my friends'.

Lack of acceptance of neurosis as 'real' illness also reduced available practical support. Thus, little help was forthcoming from husbands irritated by their wives' 'imaginary troubles'. Some of them even rendered less help than before. Thus Emma's husband, who liked a 'regimented, strictly run home', withdrew the little help he gave his wife with the children on the grounds that 'spoiling' her was clearly harmful. The weak position of wives in marital bargaining situations certainly did not help.

Most practical help came from female members of the family: mothers, sisters and adult daughters. It is a taken-for-granted assumption, in our society, that female relatives have the duty to care for the sick and dependent and they are the first to be called upon when the need arises (Blaxter, 1976; Graham, 1983). Many female relatives appeared to find it considerably easier to provide practical assistance than to give emotional support. Tasks can be carried out by people committed to doing what they perceive as their duty; they cannot show love and affection and understanding if these sentiments are missing. Interestingly, the duty to provide practical help was felt, even by those relatives who did not accord the legitimacy of sickness to the sufferer. For example, Sally's mother and sister-in-law criticised her for not 'snapping out of' depression and blamed her for neglecting her children, nevertheless they felt it their duty to help care for those 'neglected' children. Although the problem of reciprocity did not arise with these relatives, because their sense of duty outweighed any expectation of return favours, the long-term nature of the condition sometimes became a problem; when no improvement was observed offers of assistance tended to fall away.

Many women expected and found the wider kin group to be hostile rather than friendly. This reaction is frequently encountered by psychiatric patients as the contagion of stigma (and possibly the fear of some inheritable mental illness) spreads through the network. Indeed, sufferers from other stigmatised illness conditions face the rejection of their kin group, as was discussed in the previous chapter. Nevertheless, most women in the survey had some contact with cousins, in-laws and their children, but such contact was often slight, hardly more than an acknowledgement of the kin network. Typically, it was said that the wider family group met together at funerals and weddings; not many, apparently, engaged in Christmas reunions. As in the case of casual contacts with strangers, the wider kin group was of greatest value to the most isolated women, for whom it provided at least some slight feeling of belonging.

THE MEN—BY CONTRAST

The most marked difference in the social support received respectively by men and women was in its provenance. While only a third of the women regarded their husbands as the main providers of emotional support, a large majority of the men (seventeen out of twenty) ascribed this role to their wives. Moreover, these neurotic men received a more satisfactory level of support from their wives than did many of the neurotic women from their husbands.

It is a common observation that men and women are differently involved in the matter of caring for people in need and providing emotional support for family members. There is a growing literature on caring; on its practical and emotional content and on the social position and rewards of the carers. Recently, the social and economic relations which determine the status of caring have also been explored (Finch and Groves, 1983). In addition, studies of sick and disabled adults and children have described the work of those who care and look after them. One subject on which consensus exists among writers of many different affiliations and views is that care for those in need is mainly provided by women, just as the provision of emotional support for the family is seen as the women's function. In Western societies, strong cultural expectations link women with the role of caring, and Graham argues that caring relationships are those involving women; it is the presence of a woman—as a wife, mother, daughter, neighbour, friend—which marks out a relationship as, potentially at least, a caring one. (Graham, 1983, p. 15).

In Western culture women are associated with sensitivity, gentleness, an awareness of the feelings of others and expressions of love and tenderness. By contrast, the male identity is linked to being unemotional, independent, active, competitive and aggressive (Fransella and Frost, 1977). There is some controversy as to how these gender characteristics and gender expectations have developed, one suggestion being that qualities of sensitivity, understanding and caring have been necessary for women's survival in a male-dominated society. Baker Miller argues that 'feminine intuition' is the means by which women recognise the wishes, pleasures and displeasures of the dominant males. Others argue that the loving care provided by women is the result of the particular way that reproduction and the division of labour are organised in Western societies.

It is not surprising that the male sufferers from neurotic problems in the survey expected and received emotional support from their wives, since both took it for granted that this was the natural order of things. While many of the women found their husbands to be unavailable and uninterested when they tried to talk to them, the men found their wives to be just the opposite. The three men who did not rely on their wives for support described marital conflicts; all the others found their wives supportive.

As did the women in the sample, the men wanted to talk confidentially about their neurotic problems, fears and anxieties and their psychiatric treatment; these matters they were able to discuss with their wives. As said, women in general are the more inclined towards a psychiatric interpretation of problems, so it is not surprising that these wives approved of their husbands attending psychiatric treatment. Indeed some men, apparently, agreed to treatment at the insistence of their wives.

Thus, support for men appeared to be both adequate and satisfactory; it is possible, however, that men expect a lower level of emotional support than women do and that they evaluate as satisfactory the kind of support which would seem less than adequate to women. Komarovsky, for example, argued that in Western culture men suffered from a 'trained incapacity to share'. The male image is linked to the non-expression of emotion and therefore men with neurotic problems are conceivably inhibited from discussing their emotional problems with their intimates. Expressing feelings of fear, panic and vulnerability would be especially difficult, and considered unmanly.

While most women were of the opinion that no one could entirely understand their experiences and innermost feelings, most men considered that their wives were very well able to understand them. This, too, can be due to a lesser expectation as to what constitutes empathy.

Male neurotics fared less well with other members of their social networks, especially other men. They were not inclined to claim the sick role and even when doctors legitimised it by granting sick leave, they found it difficult to accept. The social group around them, in turn, was unwilling to accord them the sick role, even more so than in the case of the women. An able-bodied healthy looking man does not appear to qualify for even a modified sick role on the grounds of neurosis, and one or two of the men dealt with this problem in a curious way. They told their male intimates that they had 'wangled' a long period of sick leave by being 'clever about it' and by 'telling tall stories' to 'credulous' doctors. Apparently the role of the malingerer, able cleverly to manipulate the system, is preferable to the role of the neurotic!

The men experienced far fewer problems with practical assistance, perhaps because they needed it less than did the women in the survey. Many women needed assistance of a kind which female network members were able to and expected to provide, but the men had no corresponding need of help from members of their own sex. When they were too disturbed for work they went on sick leave. Their condition could, of course, threaten considerable work-related problems (demotion, loss of job etc.), but potentially serious as thay may have been, these problems did not result in demands on the social network. It was taken for granted that when help was needed with practical daily problems the wives were there to do it. For example, three of the men became incapacitated in ways which prevented them from driving cars and two were too depressed to work on their allotments. It appeared to be assumed by all concerned that the wives would cope, even if they had paid employment themselves. Previous research on impairment drew attention to the commonly shared assumption of families and health workers that when female relations are available there can be no problem.

6 Experiences with GPs, Psychiatrists and Other Helpers

ENCOUNTERS WITH GENERAL PRACTITIONERS

General practitioners (GPs), or family doctors, as they are often called, are consulted by people with a wide variety of problems which they perceive to be of a medical nature. Having diagnosed a problem, general practitioners must then decide whether to undertake treatment themselves or to refer the patient to one or other of the specialist services. In the United Kingdom, the majority of people diagnosed as suffering from a psychiatric illness are treated by general practitioners without recourse to the psychiatric services. According to a survey by Shepherd *et al.* (1966), London family doctors referred to psychiatrists only 5.1 per cent of the patients they diagnosed as having a psychiatric disorder. In the United States, it is not uncommon for people to consult psychiatrists directly, and a greater proportion of those who first take their emotional problems to a general practitioner are referred to psychiatrists (Goldberg and Huxley, 1980).

A number of studies have looked at patterns of psychiatric referral. They indicate considerable diversity in referral practices between general practitioners reflecting, among other things, the varying extent of their interests in providing treatment themselves and of their confidence in psychiatrists. An important research result is that many general practitioners initially treat patients with minor psychiatric disorders themselves, only referring them to psychiatrists when they fail to respond to treatment (May and Gregory, 1968; Goldberg and Huxley, 1980). Such was the experience of the majority of the respondents, men and women, in the present study, who were

115

sent to psychiatrists only after a period of treatment by their general practitioners. In fact, the only exceptions were seven patients referred by hospital doctors (four following surgery and three after taking a drug overdose), two referred by their doctor on the request of psychologists involved with their children and just three referred by their doctors after consultation and without prior treatment.

Of the patients who had been treated by their general practitioners, all but three had had tranquillisers, sedatives, or anti-depressants prescribed for them; two others said that their doctors had conducted psychotherapy sessions. This confirmed other research findings that only a small proportion of family doctors attempt psychiatric treatment other than the prescription of psychotropic drugs (Shepherd *et al.,* 1966; Goldberg and Huxley, 1980).

Patients finding themselves referred to psychiatrists after a period of general practitioner treatment and the continuous or intermittent use of drugs, tend to regard referral as an indication of the failure of that treatment. This was true of the study respondents who, with a few exceptions, were very critical of their doctors' attempts to help them.

It is notoriously difficult for researchers to evaluate the degree of patients' satisfaction and dissatisfaction with medical services. Several writers on research methodology have argued that more sensitive techniques are needed than those presently in use, but just as important is the problem of defining the meaning of satisfaction in this context. Stimson and Webb (1975), in their study of the consultation process in general practice, pointed out that people's feelings about their doctors fluctuate from one encounter to the next, and that they may feel satisfied with some aspects of their doctor's actions, while being perturbed about others.

Not only will such feelings change over time, but even after a single consultation a patient interviewed cannot contain all the varying elements of that encounter under a label such as 'satisfied' or 'dissatisfied'. To sum up and label in this way distorts reality and misses the continual process of ordering and evaluation which is going on. (p. 77).

Patients' referral to psychiatrists did not terminate their

contact with family doctors who continued to treat them for other problems and, indeed, for their neurotic ones once psychiatric treatment had ended. At both first and second interviews, respondents discussed their experiences with regard to general practitioners' handling of their neurotic problems and in the majority of instances the verdict was that they were unhelpful (Table 6.1). It must be emphasised that these responses were specific to the doctors' performance in dealing with neurotic problems and additional comments made by the same respondents indicated confidence in their doctors' ability in other areas: e.g. 'doctor was very good when baby was sick', and 'he was marvellous when my husband had the accident'.

Table 6.1: Perceptions of General Practitioners' performance in providing help with neurosis

	Women	Men
Helpful	5	3
Unhelpful	50	14
Mixed	10	3
Total	65	20

Some 12 per cent of the respondents (seven women and three men) were antagonistic towards the medical profession generally and amongst them were those with the most severe social problems. For example Peggy, who had to struggle with her eighteen-year-old spastic twins, two other children and a chronically sick husband with addiction problems, displayed a longstanding hostility to doctors of all kinds. Similarly Laura, who had lived in very poor housing for many years with her three young children and a husband, who lost a leg in an industrial accident and became permanently unemployed, made quite vitriolic comments about doctors in general. It is of interest that similar findings were recorded by Mildred Blaxter (1976), in her study of physically disabled people. She noted a strong correlation between the presence of social problems and a poor relationship with general practitioners and found that there was a 'small but clearly distinguishable group of families themselves defined by social welfare agencies as "problems" who were likely to be on bad terms with their GPs' (p. 212). People such as Peggy and Laura had a long history of dealings with medical and social services which seemed to them uniformly unhelpful.

Table 6.2: *Main criticism of General Practitioners*

Nature of Criticism	Women n = 65	Men n = 20
Lacks skills to treat neurosis	38	7
Prescribes drugs too often, or thoughtlessly	36	8
Dismisses or minimises problems	33	—
Does not give enough information	28	10
Does not allow enough time	28	8
Unsympathetic to neurotics	22	—
Made psychiatric referral at wrong time or for wrong reason	18	9

However, the majority of those who found their doctors unhelpful showed no hostility towards them nor to the medical profession generally. The most frequently mentioned criticism of general practitioners are listed in Table 6.2; these criticisms are not mutually exclusive, most of the respondents having criticised their GPs on more than one count. That they lacked the skills to treat neurosis was frequently alleged, a finding of particular interest in the light of other studies which indicate that lay people tend not to criticise doctors' clinical skills and competence. For example, in studies of doctors and patients, Cartwright and her colleagues found repeatedly that when considering sources of dissatisfaction, people referred to doctors' manners, personality, accessibility or interest, but not to their clinical knowledge or skills (Cartwright, 1967; Cartwright and Anderson, 1981). In another study of general practice Jefferys and Sachs (1983) found that most patients talked readily about their doctors' inter-personal skills and some also referred to their efficiency and thoroughness, but hardly anyone mentioned medical capability. These researchers and others argued that patients take doctors' professional knowledge and skills for granted, assuming that these are inherent in medical qualifications and that lay people do not feel themselves able to judge clinical competence (Roberts, 1985). Respondents of the present study were, therefore, untypical. Comments such as 'he doesn't know enough about depression' and 'my doctor hasn't got the know-how to treat nerve cases' were made frequently.

Prescribing habits also came in for a lot of criticism. Common to many of the respondents was the view that drugs are too often prescribed for neurotic problems, and general practitioners were blamed for concentrating on drug solutions. Respondents referred to their 'thoughtlessness' in prescribing, their 'inadequate knowledge' of drugs and their failure to monitor patients' responses to drugs; insufficient knowledge of dosage and of side-effects were also suggested. Certainly, the large number of repeat prescriptions, issued apparently without checking and monitoring, gave the impression of carelessness, as did the alleged habit of some doctors of writing prescriptions 'within a minute or two' of the patient's arrival in the consulting room.

The criticism that general practitioners have an inadequate knowledge of drugs was fostered by two further factors: first, when referring to psychiatrists, some general practitioners were reported as saying 'I'll send you to a specialist who knows more about drugs' or words to that effect; and second, psychiatrists when first encountering the patients often changed their prescriptions, making such comments as 'this will be better for you', implying inferior knowledge on the part of the general practitioners.

Whilst criticisms of treatment skills and of prescribing habits came from both male and female patients, allegations that doctors minimised their complaints and lacked sympathy came only from the women, who felt, in addition, that they were given a prescription in order to be rid of them, rather than because the prescribed drugs were the appropriate treatment.

Sandra, 32, two children 5 and 12: 'Dr. M said I was worrying about nothing. He was very casual at first, then he started to say it is probably a delayed reaction to childbirth. He said many women feel like this. He gave me tranquillisers, he wanted to get rid of me'.

Several women said that doctors explained their troubles as

'usual women's problems', due variously to childbirth, menopause, menstruation, or childlessness. It seemed to the women receiving such explanations that inherent in them were dismissiveness and the trivialisation of their problems, which were regarded, by doctors, as 'part of nature' or as 'over-reaction'.

Janet, 47, five children between 10 and 28: 'Dr. D just said it was my age and the change. I told him I didn't think it was that because I still have periods. Then he said it could be the children leaving home, the nest emptying, but I told him my youngest son is only ten. He didn't want to know, just put me down as a nuisance. He is an efficient doctor, but doesn't like nerve cases'.

Becky, 21, no children: 'The doctor just said I would feel better when I had a baby. He didn't take me seriously. He said there are many women like me, it is not unusual. He just gave me tranquillisers'.

Why was it that only the women complained of cursory treatment by doctors and of their readiness to write a prescription in order to be rid of them? It was not that the men were uncritical of their doctors' performance, so the gender difference here requires another explanation. It seems likely that the women's impression of not being taken seriously arose out of their doctors' linking of depression and other neurotic problems to their reproductive processes saying or implying that such experiences were part of 'being a woman'. It is true that many of the women made the same link themselves (see Table 2.3, Chapter 2), but they regarded their problems as serious even while attributing them, at least partly, to hormone changes.

It is possible that doctors were seeking to reassure their patients and that remarks such as 'it is natural to feel like this' and 'many women have these problems' were directed to that end. To the women concerned, however, such observations conveyed not comfort but a feeling of being dismissed.

The other criticism exclusive to the women was that doctors were unsympathetic towards their problems. It seemed to the women that doctors disliked neurotic patients and also disliked treating neurotic problems such as depression, panic and phobias and their attendant physical disorders such as headaches and sleeplessness. They came to this conclusion because the same doctors seemed sympathetic and full of understanding on other occasions.

There is certainly some evidence that many general practitioners prefer treating physical illnesses to emotional problems and more serious conditions to the seemingly trivial ones (Stimson, 1976; Cartwright and Anderson, 1981). Nevertheless, this cannot be the whole explanation, because similar problems presented by male patients appeared to have been taken more seriously: none of the men mentioned lack of sympathy, although they were critical of other aspects of their doctors' performance. The problems of men may have been more sympathetically regarded and taken more seriously because they disrupted paid employment. As discussed earlier, men saw their various problems as mostly work-related (with regard to both cause and consequence) and they presented problems to doctors in this light. It became apparent from interviews with the men that they thought doctors sympathetic to problems which might disrupt employment.

Another criticism of general practitioners, voiced by both men and women, concerned lack of information. It is a common research finding that patients complain of receiving inadequate information from their doctors (Stimson and Webb, 1975; Cartwright and Anderson, 1981). The tenor of such complaints is that doctors are unwilling to divulge details of medical conditions and regard lay people as being unable to understand medical information. Corroborative evidence was obtained from the respondents in this study; they complained of inadequate briefing concerning the drugs they were taking, their purpose and their side-effects, if any; they said that they were given insufficient information as to why they were referred, who the specialists were and what they would do; doctors were less than frank and did not prepare them adequately for psychiatric treatment.

Marion, 33: 'The doctor told me that he would send me to a specialist who knew about drugs. He never used the word psychiatrist. I saw from the card that I had to go to S.

Hospital [local General Hospital] but I still didn't know that my appointment was with a mental specialist. It was a shock. The doctor should have explained it, he should have told me'.

A related criticism, expressed by respondents of both sexes, was that doctors did not devote enough time to them and that consequently they were unable fully to explain their troubles. Of course, it can be said that these particular patients had a special need to talk at length about their problems, a need that doctors could not satisfy however much time they were prepared to spend with the patient. However, other studies show similar feelings on the part of non-neurotic general practice patients. Thus, Jefferys and Sachs (1983) writing about patients in general practice noted that 'what they often wanted was an opportunity to present the problem in all its complexity to the doctor, in the expectation that he or she would have the knowledge, skill and sympathy to show them how to deal with it' (p. 303). This exactly expressed the feelings of respondents here: there was no chance to talk.

Respondents commented with mixed feelings on the general practitioners' decision to refer them to psychiatrists. Some said that if the doctor is unable to help, it is right to call in a specialist, and a minority (ten) said either that they asked for referral or would have done if the doctor hadn't suggested it because they had lost confidence in the doctor's ability to help.

Helen, 52: 'I asked Dr. B to send me to a specialist. I wanted to talk to somebody who knew about these things, who could tell me what the trouble was. I wanted to know if I am imagining things, if I am going mental, I wanted to understand. Dr. B was kind and patient but he couldn't explain, he couldn't do anything'.

However, to the majority it was a shock to find themselves referred to psychiatrists, especially if inadequately prepared (see above), and GPs were blamed for the way they handled referrals. Criticisms were expressed of the timing, either on the grounds that it should have been done earlier ('He should have known it was not going to work') or later ('He could have tried a bit longer').

The point was also made that general practitioners became impatient and irritated when there was no improvement, blamed patients for lack of treatment success and referred them to psychiatrists in consequence. Blame was communicated by the doctor: straightforwardly, 'he said I was not trying enough, that I didn't want to conquer the trouble', or by implication, 'Dr. L said we were not getting anywhere and that the best would be to send me to a psychiatrist; maybe I would open up more with somebody else. He said the psychiatrist might get me out of the house. He was very pleasant but I felt awful, I felt that I failed somehow . . . that if I tried more, I wouldn't be a disappointment to him'. Referral in such cases was perceived as a punishment.

It is likely that subsequent experiences with psychiatrists coloured patients' feelings concerning their referrals (first interviews were conducted after patients had met with psychiatrists); those who found psychiatric treatment helpful were more likely to assess the general practitioners' decision to refer in a positive light than were those whose view of the treatment was negative. Encounters with general practitioners were also reassessed in the light of perceptions of improvements (or vice-versa): those who felt better by the time of the second interview were also likely to express more positive views about their doctors.

It was of interest that the minority of respondents who found the general practitioners to be helpful with their neurotic problems, commented favourably on their patience, willingness to listen and other inter-personal skills; none mentioned technical skills as a positive benefit.

ENCOUNTERS WITH PSYCHIATRISTS

For many patients, psychiatric treatment can start with a sense of failure, shame and betrayal; this was described by Goffman (1961) referring to persons admitted to mental hospitals. People referred to psychiatrists with neurotic problems also have a sense of failure and shame on first meeting them: to patients' self-perception as inadequate ('I can't cope') are added perceptions of having failed to improve while receiving treatment in a general practice setting.

It was during the second interviews, a year after they first met psychiatrists, that respondents discussed their experiences of these specialists. More of both women and men found psychiatrists helpful than was the case in respect of the general practitioners. More, also, expressed mixed feelings and there were correspondingly fewer 'unhelpful' verdicts.

Table 6.3: Perceptions of psychiatrists' performance

	Women	Men
Helpful	25	6
Unhelpful	25	8
Mixed	15	6
Total	65	20

Why were the psychiatrists viewed in a more positive light than the general practitioners? Firstly, the psychiatrists devoted more time to their patients, allowing them to talk at length and showing more interest in their problems. Most of those who found the psychiatrists helpful, and even most of those whose feelings about them were mixed, commented favourably on the length of time that these specialists spent with them, compared with the few minutes accorded them by their family doctor, and on the much greater interest shown in their personal problems. Secondly, although the psychiatrist prescribed drugs, patients gained the impression that these were ancillary to the main treatment which centred upon talks. Psychiatrists' careful and knowledgeable handling of drugs was contrasted favourably with the general practitioners' method of prescribing. Thirdly, a minority had forced themselves to believe in the psychiatrists because they could perceive no other source of help. For them, psychiatrists were regarded as a last resort; as specialists they had to have the best knowledge available and the thought that they could not help was too frightening to contemplate. This was the view of Kate who said:

'The psychiatrist is the specialist in this field. If he cannot help nobody can. You've got to believe that he will help you, just got to believe it, otherwise you lose all hope'.

It should, perhaps, be remarked that this research was concerned only with patients who had been referred to psychiatrists and that, obviously, only those patients could hold contrasting views of the performance of family doctors and psychiatrists. An overall survey of neurotic patients' opinions of family doctors and psychiatrists might not confirm the bias in favour of the latter reported here. Even so, it is undoubtedly true that psychiatrists can devote more time to their patients. Indeed, such is the nature of their treatment, they have to.

However, despite favourable comparisons with general practitioners, several criticisms of the psychiatrists were expressed, perhaps the most important of which was that they reformulated and re-interpreted the patients' problems in such a way as to distort the original statement. This was typically a problem experienced by the women, many of whom related their problems, as they saw them, only to find that psychiatrists discounted their formulation of what was wrong. Women who thought that their problem was loneliness, or the hardships of life, or female biological processes, had their thoughts directed to their relationships with their husbands and children, to their own childhood experiences, or to their innermost worries and fears. Some of the women accepted this reformulation, or at least conceded that 'there may be something in it' but to others it seemed that instead of helping with the 'real' problem, psychiatrists wanted to discuss issues which seemed, to the women, to be unimportant or irrelevant. A succinct and blunt expression of these divergent perspectives came from May:

'I wanted to tell him about our flat having no bathroom, and my mother half-paralysed after her stroke and *he* wanted to talk about my marriage. I could see there was no help there, after only two sessions'.

Even when there was agreement on the core of the problem and the way discussions should go, patient and psychiatrist could find themselves at odds. Kim and her psychiatrist concurred that her problem was rooted in her marriage but while

Table 6.4: Sources of dissatisfaction with psychiatrists

Criticisms	Women n = 65	Men n = 20
Reformulation and re-interpretation of the problem	42	2
Disbelief in patients' views	27	—
Use of technical language	23	6
Abrupt termination of treatment	28	8
Personality, manner or approach of psychiatrist	21	9

Kim felt that physical and verbal abuse by her husband was the cause and wanted advice on how to get out of the trap of marriage to a violent man who was, nevertheless, the father of her two children, the psychiatrist looked elsewhere, asking why she permitted the violence and probing to discover whether, perhaps, she took pleasure in it.

The argument of psychiatrists has always been that patients are reluctant to face up to the root of their emotional problems, preferring to concentrate on shallow issues and practical difficulties, and that it is much easier to blame another person that to ask oneself hurtful and uncomfortable questions. A patient's unwillingness to discuss the issues raised by the psychiatrist is professionally interpreted as 'a reluctance to face the problem' but to the patient the psychiatrist, in refusing to help with the real issue, is the unwilling one.

In many cases, the prior discussions with general practitioners contributed to mistaken expectations of the likely course of psychiatric treatment. The women had given much thought to their emotional problems and had even come to some general agreement with their doctors concerning them; now the psychiatrist wanted to start afresh and reformulate the problem. They felt strongly that their hard-won explanations were discredited by the psychiatrist.

A closely related source of dissatisfaction for women, but not for men, was the feeling that psychiatrists did not believe what they said. Their statements were not so much re-interpreted as disbelieved; for example, when women described the side-effects of drugs, or withdrawal symptoms on giving them up, they were frequently told that they were mistaken. When women explained the hours needed to nurse relatives or clean the house, they met with disbelief. (Previous studies also reported psychiatrists disbelieving women's descriptions of their lives: see Smith and David, 1975).

It was interesting to observe, on the basis of the interviews, that men do not share this feeling of being disbelieved, and that neither do they complain, to anything like the same extent as women, of the re-interpretation of their problems by psychiatrists. It is possible that psychiatrists, in this research predominantly male, are more inclined to accept the statements and interpretations of their male patients; a male psychiatrist may be more in sympathy with a male patient who complains of work-related problems than with a female patient who locates her trouble in domestic worries. Another possibility is that men, having thought less deeply about their emotions, arrive in the consulting room without any clear-cut interpretations of the nature of their problems. Also, men are less accustomed to having their statements and reports questioned and doubted than are women, and possibly are less likely to feel that psychiatrists are doing so.

Another difficulty experienced by the respondents was the use of medical language by psychiatrists. The translation of lay descriptions into technical nomenclature was disliked and distrusted. As *Sally, 28,* put it: 'They have their own words for everything so that it sounds different'.

It is true that doctors generally employ technical terms, and write prescriptions, which are incomprehensible to many of their patients. People become accustomed to this experience with regard to physical illness but they may, nevertheless, be disconcerted to have their personal feelings and problems described as 'anxiety neurosis', 'acute frustration', or 'hostility to self', expressions quoted by respondents as coming from psychiatrists.

Technical terminology and the reformulation of problems, i.e. a change from a lay to a psychiatric focus, can give rise to feelings of guilt and shame in people who cannot understand what the psychiatrists says and cannot grasp the meaning of the psychiatric perspective. In fact, women who could not comprehend what the specialist was getting at tended to blame themselves for their failure to understand. They felt that they had not tried hard enough or had subconsciously resisted what was being put to them.

Alice, 33: 'I am a disappointment to him, I can see that. I cannot understand what he is getting at . . . he has his own way of saying things. If he could only explain better it would help . . . when he starts explaining what depression is, I am lost and then I think I am stupid. I feel awful. What is a frustration, anyway'?

Liz, 29: 'Dr. D gives such involved explanations that often I can't follow his meaning. I did a year's psychology and I should know the terms he uses, but often I sit there and feel lost. It sounds so complex and involved and I wonder if it's my fault for blocking out . . . maybe I don't understand because unconsciously I don't want to . . .'.

Another contentious issue is that psychiatrists can terminate treatment when they judge it appropriate, not when the patients wish it. Those who find the psychiatrist unhelpful may wish for more effort or a different approach; those who find the sessions helpful may well want to continue them. Some respondents felt abandoned when psychiatrists, often without prior notice, told them not to come any more; they had no one left to turn to.

Psychiatrists frequently make the point that it is no part of their function to allow their patients to become dependent upon them; indeed to do so would represent a negation of the very thing they are striving to achieve. However, to decide at what stage a state of dependence has, or is about to, come about is not easy and it is hardly surprising if the views of psychiatrist and patient do not always concur, the one saying that requests for continuing psychiatric help are a sign of dependence; the other, that to stop the sessions before a solution or at least a fair measure of improvement is achieved, is unhelpful.

Hilary, 42: 'He said that we had to stop before I became dependent on talks with him; I was not to go anymore. But I said "how do you know I will become dependent?, you might as well say that I'll be dependent on my GP"'.

It is a sign of the unequal power of the two participants, psychiatrist and patient, that the former invariably has the last word on the continuance of the treatment. The patient, of course, can take the decision to discontinue treatment, but cannot persevere with it if the psychiatrist deems otherwise.

The personality, manner and approach of psychiatrists was another area of criticism. Words like 'cold', 'hard', and 'unfeeling' were applied to some of them, others were said to lack understanding and interest. Patients' comments were, somewhat naturally, coloured by their perceptions of the success or failure of the therapy: twelve patients ended psychiatric treatment themselves because they found it unhelpful.

Comments concerning treatment methods came from only a few of the respondents. Individual treatment by psychiatrists on a one-to-one basis was preferred to other forms of treatment such as group therapy and attendance at day centres. Indeed, there was an assumption that arrangements for group treatment were made mainly because psychiatrists had too little time for individual therapy.

WOMEN GENERAL PRACTITIONERS AND PSYCHIATRISTS

The medical profession is preponderantly male, and female patients, perforce, are usually in the situation of having to consult male doctors. Would the large number of women who suffer from depression, phobias and other neurotic problems fare better if they were treated by women doctors? It has been argued that women doctors, treating members of their own sex, share with them the female experience and thus are better able than male doctors to empathise and care for them, a proposition often put forward in the areas of gynaecology and obstetrics (Roberts, 1981B). Similarly, it can be argued that in cases where neurotic illness is centred upon the social experience of being a housewife or mother (often both) or on a biological event, such as a miscarriage or the menopause, a woman doctor would be better able to understand the patients' complaints.

In the present study there were only two instances of women

general practitioners treating women and eventually referring them for psychiatry although there were, additionally, one or two female 'locums'. Among the psychiatrists, also, only two were women, a small percentage of the female respondents being numbered among their patients. No hard conclusions could be drawn from these few woman-to-woman relationships but nevertheless the opportunity was taken to test patient reactions in these circumstances. Far from preferring them, the female respondents were scathing in their criticisms of the women doctors they had encountered:

Julie, 30, two children 5 and 7: 'The psychiatrist was a woman and I couldn't talk to her. She was not married and she didn't understand about husbands and children . . . she didn't have the experience. Her life-style was completely different from mine. For example, she asked me why I thought I had to cook every day, why this was important to me. She didn't understand, she asked silly questions like this'.

June, 35, four children 2, 8, 13 and 16: 'The psychiatrist was a young woman, she was too young to understand. She asked irrelevant questions. She thought I was a nuisance. I couldn't tell her anything. She made me feel silly and petty'.

Fiona, 29, three children 3, 9 and 11: 'My doctor is a lady doctor and she is very unsympathetic. I can feel it when I try to tell her anything . . . she thinks I am a nuisance. Once she said it was time I sorted myself out. I wish I could change her for a man; they are more sympathetic. Women can get very hard when they have a career'.

Of course, complaints of doctors' lack of sympathy and inability to understand were frequently made in respect of male doctors, the point of interest here being that women doctors were not thought to be different in this respect. Perhaps it was easier to deal with male doctors who could not be expected to share female biological and social experiences than with women doctors, who, insofar as they shared them, had manifestly overcome the attendant difficulties. The several references to women doctors being too young were matched by only one such criticism in respect of their male counterparts.

Other studies have obtained broadly similar findings. For example, many middle-aged women patients in Helen Roberts' study (1985) preferred male doctors. Trying to account for this preference, Roberts suggested that it may be culturally more acceptable to appear 'weak' in front of a man. It may well be true that a neurotic woman, not coping too well and finding herself confronted by an obviously successful member of her own sex, thereby has her sense of inadequacy heightened, whereas in front of a male doctor she can adopt the traditional 'weaker-sex' posture.

There is also the possibility that the female general practitioners and psychiatrists encountered by the women were genuinely less sympathetic than their male counterparts. A woman doctor, writing about her experiences, made the point that women had to be tougher than men in order to succeed in the male-dominated medical world (Young, 1981) and, having fought many battles themselves, may lack sympathy for women neurotics whom they regard as unwilling to fight.

The reason for women preferring male doctors may also lie in the social stereotype of 'doctor' as a man; reality (in the shape of a female doctor) clashing with expectation, based on stereotype, can be an uncomfortable experience.

THE PROBLEMS OF DRUG-TAKING

Every one of the eighty-five respondents in this study had been prescribed tranquillisers, sedatives or anti-depressants during the course of their treatment and they expressed a range of views concerning their effectiveness and the problems attendant upon using them, there being a wide measure of consensus on the dangers associated with long-term drug usage.

By the time of the second interviews, a year after psychiatric referral, all of the respondents had gained considerable experience of taking one or other psychotropic drug. The pattern that revealed itself was of the usefulness of drugs when they were first prescribed and a diminution of confidence in them as time passed and no long-lasting benefit was perceived.

Side-effects posed a major problem; the majority of the

women mentioned drowsiness and tiredness which they ascribed to the drugs. The following comment was typical:

> *Jill, 22:* 'I couldn't think straight, it's as though my mind was blocked off. I forgot everything I was so tired. When I stopped taking them I could think again, I was alert and remembered things'.

It is by no means easy for patients, or even doctors, to separate the symptoms of a neurotic illness from the side-effects of the drugs. For example, depression is said to be characterised by fatigue and inertia (Litman, 1978) and most of the women in the study were depressed, even those whose problem was classified differently. In such circumstances there may well be doubt as to whether drowsiness and sluggishness are due to the condition or to the treatment. Certainly, many of the respondents were convinced that drugs worsened their condition in this respect.

Other side-effects complained of were nausea and sickness, bad nights and nightmares. One said, 'I'm struggling to wake up and can't'. Others reported experiences of a like nature.

After taking drugs for a lengthy period, trying to come off them, or even to reduce the dosage, constituted a severe difficulty; many had tried and failed to do without them. They were afraid not to have their tablets in the house.

> *June, 35:* 'Valium isn't the answer but by the time you find out you can't give it up. Doctors don't know what withdrawal means, they don't believe me when I try to explain. Even the loss of one tablet can be a disaster'.

Women with children had special problems. They were fearful that by becoming drowsy or forgetful they could expose their infants to some harm; there was also the fear that the children might imitate drug-taking and grow up thinking, falsely, that drugs are the answer to problems.

A variety of medicine-taking patterns were followed and in general medical advice as to the proper dosage tended to be disregarded. Especially was this the case with those who had been prescribed the same drug over a lengthy period; they had formed their own opinion regarding the amount they should take and the frequency with which they should take it. Sandra was confident that she knew, better than the doctor, how to use her tranquilliser and without consulting him, had tried to cut down, taking the drug only when she knew that she had to:

> 'I know when I must take it but most of the time it is just there and gives me reassurance. I've managed to cut down but I still get the prescription in case I need more'.

Not only was medicine-taking not always in accordance with doctors' advice, it was often haphazard. Although some respondents tried systematically to reduce the dose, others consumed their prescribed tablets unsystematically, being unsure of quantities and frequency. An example was Peggy who said that she grabbed a tranquilliser when she needed it, day or night, doubled the dose when there was more family trouble than usual and forgot to take it at all when things were calmer. Some discontinued or reduced their consumption of drugs when they experienced side-effects and stepped it up once the side-effects disappeared.

Lay opinion was often sought and the advice obtained influenced the pattern of medicine-taking. Women, especially, like to discuss such matters among themselves and there is no doubt that in recent years a considerable body of lay experience regarding the use of tranquillisers has accumulated. Many of the respondent women were acquainted with others who had taken these drugs or others like them, for example, sleeping pills (often on prescription by a general practitioner), and the practice, at least in their circles, appeared to be fairly common and quite acceptable, as long as no psychiatrist was involved. Thus, access to the experience of their social groups had been available to female respondents prior to referral and, if the fact of their psychiatric treatment could be concealed, would continue to be. This informal process was evidenced by remarks made by these respondents; one said that a friend told her to take only one tablet at night because two would make her drowsy the next morning, another was advised to double the dose at bedtime when it would do no harm, and so on.

ALTERNATIVE SOURCES OF HELP

Besides general practitioners and psychiatrists, help with neurotic problems is available from a surprisingly wide range of sources within the formal network of professional helpers and organised self-help groups. On the whole, these 'alternative' sources were regarded by respondents as being more effective than either general practitioners or psychiatrists.

Table 6.5: Alternative sources of help

Helping Agencies	Number of respondents in contact with help sources	
	Women n = 65	*Men* n = 20
Social workers	28	3
Health visitors	21	—
Marriage guidance/family counsellors	13	—
Self-help groups (Agoraphobia Society, Scope etc.)	13	—
Samaritans	10	-
Hypnotherapists	8	1
Vicar/priest	7	—
Private psychoanalyst or psychotherapist	7	2
Physiotherapists/other hospital staff	6	1
Others (e.g. psychosexual clinic)	6	2
Number of patients who had recourse to one or more alternative helpers	41	6

Mothers with babies or young children were, or had been, routinely visited by health visitors, who were generally viewed as being helpful. The women said that they could talk to health visitors at greater length than they could to doctors and received much help from them. The neurosis of mothers comes only coincidentally within the ambit of health visitors but the women concerned felt that they could talk to them about their problems. Their presence in the home, chatting informally over a cup of tea, was contrasted favourably with the unfamiliar, and sometimes rather daunting, atmosphere of the consulting room.

Moreover, these conversations took place in the course of routine 'baby visits'; the women did not feel themselves labelled 'neurotics' or 'non-copers' and the doctor/patient syndrome was absent. Health visitors and nurses at day hospitals and day centres were the only professionals with a nursing background to be involved with respondents, none of whom had contact with psychiatric or community nurses.

If perhaps less well-regarded than health visitors, social workers, too, were seen as supportive. Housing problems, unemployment in the family and difficulties with teenage children were among the problems that had led to contact with social workers, but in the course of subsequent discussions the emotional problems surrounding these other difficulties were ventilated. There were also eight women who received counselling from social workers on the suggestion of their doctors. As with the health visitors, social workers talked to people in their homes and appeared to be in less of a hurry than were the doctors; their inter-personal skills and ability to counsel in depth were regarded as helpful. However, some reservations were expressed on the grounds that involvement with welfare services labelled families as 'non-copers' and some women were apprehensive of the supposed power of social workers to take children away from mothers who were 'psychiatric cases'.

Opinions of the performance of psychotherapists and psychoanalysts, to whom only a few of the respondents had access, were mixed, and not necessarily typical in view of the small number of cases. However, Diane, an agoraphobic, was most appreciative of her psychoanalyst: 'She arranges to meet me on the street so as to get me out of the house and walks back with me; she is really excellent'. This specialist was attached to a general practice, an uncommon arrangement.

The most uniform enthusiasm and the least ambivalence was for those sources of help which are not part of the statutory medical, psychiatric or social services, even if not all the respondents availed themselves thereof. The Samaritans provided much assistance to very depressed women and to agoraphobics by talking to them on the telephone at great length and offering to send tapes relevant to their problems. Marriage guidance and family counsellors were also helpful to women, if less readily available than the Samaritans, although they wanted to meet the husbands, who, typically, were reluctant to accompany their wives to counselling sessions. The Church had proved a source of help to seven of the women all of whom said that they had lost touch with their church but had returned to it when they were troubled.

There exists a variety of trained helpers who offer assistance with emotional problems on a fee-paying basis. Among these, psychoanalysts, psychotherapists and hypnotherapists were all judged to be helpful:

> *Colin Finney:* 'The hypnotherapist was the only one who helped me. I think it is money well spent to go to a private man. Even if you haven't got money to spare, it is better to manage it somehow and get help'.

> *Helen, 52:* 'If you go privately, you know there is time to talk, you don't have to hurry. You don't feel like you have to apologise for your problem being smaller than those of others who are in the waiting room'.

Private therapy sessions could continue without 'fear of being abandoned' by the specialist and without anxiety over 'wasting the doctor's time'.

Of the self-help groups the Agoraphobia Society was the only one used by more than one or two women (no man turned to these groups) and they found it extremely helpful. It was a great relief to the seven agoraphobics who became members to find others with similar problems and a forum where meetings could take place. The non-medical setting was much appreciated. It is interesting that when respondents consulted their doctors about self-help groups they met with discouragement: general practitioners advised patients not to get involved with 'unprofessional' or 'amateur' groups who can 'cause damage'. For example:

> *Iris, 24:* 'My doctor said it would only depress me to meet agoraphobics: he said these groups can't help, they only meet to feel sorry for themselves'.

Whether or not this attitude is widespread among doctors, it was interesting to discover that hardly any of those respondents who made use of private therapists or self-help groups revealed it to their doctors.

It was interesting to learn that hospital doctors other than psychiatrists can prove to be a source of alternative help. Individual specialists (e.g. an ENT consultant, an ophthalmic surgeon, and a cardiac specialist) gave considerable help with problems of depression and anxiety. Of course they were primarily consulted for their specialist services and not for neurotic illness, nevertheless some consultants were interested to discuss the emotional problems of their patients: 'The throat specialist did me more good than the psychiatrist. I was so relieved after he talked to me, I felt so much better, that I threw out all the drugs from the medicine chest'. Psychotherapists and speech therapists also proved willing to enter into conversation with patients on emotional problems. Obviously only those neurotic patients who have physical problems in addition, can have access to specialists in other areas of medicine; to the extent that these specialists are able to reassure patients regarding those physical problems, their depression or anxiety may be eased.

Discussions with hospital specialists relating to neurotic problems were not mentioned to psychiatrists or GPs, indeed the feeling was that it would have been 'tactless' to praise, for example, the advice received from the ENT specialist about depression, to a psychiatrist.

There were a number of reasons for alternative sources of help being seen so much more positively by respondents than were the psychiatrists and general practitioners.

The clinical setting of the consulting room is less conducive to talks about personal problems than is the domestic hearth which provides the background for discussions with health visitors and social workers. The consulting room is the territory of the doctor or the psychiatrist, it evidences the superior power of the help-provider and emphasises the suppliant role of the help-seeker, who can feel daunted and uncomfortable. On home territory the patient can feel less intimidated.

The appointment system, whether for the half-hour session with a psychiatrist, or the average six or seven minutes GP consultation, regulates the time available for discussion and makes patients edgy: 'By the time I can think of things I want to say, the session is finished'. Health visitors and social workers also have to operate within tight schedules but the informal home atmosphere can render this less apparent.

The social distance between lay people on the one hand and health visitors, social workers and counsellors, on the other is less marked than that between lay people and psychiatrists. This statement may not be generally applicable but it was certainly true of most of the respondents of this research, who found it easier to relax and unburden their problems with non-medical professionals: 'the psychiatrist is too high-powered for ordinary, small problems, like mine'. These helpers do not employ esoteric terminology nor do they reformulate problems in a way that some people may find unintelligible.

With regard to the 'other' specialists (ophthalmic surgeon, physiotherapist, etc.) who were reportedly so helpful, they too, were seen in the clinical setting which many patients found off-putting in other situations. Perhaps the 'success' of these specialists is to be found in the impromptu, unpremeditated nature of such discussions; patients did not have to marshal their thoughts or plan what they were going to say; an unexpected rapport encourages confidence. It may also be that the ability of these specialists to reassure patients about their physical problems led to their being seen as helpful, even though any lasting improvement in the neurotic condition was more problematic.

Private therapists also meet their patients on a different footing than do the GPs and psychiatrists of the National Health Service. Patients who seek them out and pay for their services do not feel in quite the powerless position of those who have to rely on the public sector (and who tend to lose sight of the fact that they, too, have paid for what they are getting); the private patient retains a measure of control over the situation. Too few of the respondents were treated privately for any generalisation to be possible, but there was no disillusionment among those respondents, and a number of others considered turning to the private sector in the future. Whether justified or not, some people expect private treatment to be better and worth paying for, if that is at all possible.

It can be argued that private therapy has to be actively sought out and organised and that only those who are functioning reasonably well can avail themselves (financial considerations apart) of this kind of treatment. By contrast, the Samaritans are available to the most troubled, and self-help groups also do their best to reach people who badly need help. The company of fellow-sufferers, the exchange of information and ideas of practical value ('try going out with a dog', 'carry a stick or an umbrella with you') and just discussing difficulties with equals, can provide relief.

Thus, a number of agencies can be approached and utilised by people with neurotic problems. The informal, unorganised character of some of these agencies is at once a strength and a weakness; they enable people to talk with advisers of their own choosing instead of being confronted by those impersonally chosen by the medical services; on the other hand, the whereabouts, indeed the existence of these sources of aid are not known to everyone. The effort required to seek help and to comply carefully with advice needs precisely the initiative that the neurotic may well lack. Those most in need are the most likely to miss out.

7 Who Gets Better and Why?

A SOCIOLOGICAL VIEW OF NEUROSIS

This study began with the selection of eighty-five persons whose common denominator was their social situation of having been referred for psychiatric treatment and being diagnosed as neurotic. During the study, much was learned about their work, both domestic and paid, their relationships with their families and friends, their interpretation of their problems and their encounters with professionals. In what sense could it be said that these people were 'neurotic' and how did they come to be so labelled?

From a sociological perspective, the answers seem to lie in a particular interplay of individual problems and coping mechanisms, determined by the prevalent social relations of contemporary society and by current medical and psychiatric practices. The women, who formed the majority of the respondents, and the men too, had almost all experienced considerable problems of one sort or another, related to their marriages and other family relationships or to employment, domestic and paid. These problems, not necessarily more severe than those afflicting others, appeared, in these respondents, to be linked with their neurotic condition.

Could it be said that the neurotic problems of the women and men of the research were brought about by their marital or other difficulties? Any assertion to this effect must allow that some pre-disposing factor might have contributed to those difficulties; after all, others cope with problems no less severe. Levels of tolerance vary between individuals: some can sustain a degree of pain that others would find unbearable; one person can deal cheerfully with a workload that would produce stress in another. Adversity brings out the best in some people and prostrates others. Demands on physical and mental resources of individuals can increase to breaking-point, at which stage mental or physical illness may intervene. The process is likely to be protracted as problems mount and ever-increasing efforts to cope with them prove unavailing, until the only stratagem for coping left is a breakdown. For the research women, the pattern was one of slowly deteriorating situations and vain attempts to cope, culminating in responses later termed 'neurotic'. From the evidence of this research, neurosis is a response to conditions which the individual finds intolerable and, as will be seen, it is susceptible to improvement by the amelioration of those conditions.

Depression was the most common response to the situation in which respondents found themselves and, along with phobias, obsessions and anxiety led eventually to their being caught up in current medical and psychiatric practices whereby they were provisionally labelled by their GPs as having psychological problems, were prescribed drugs and later referred to psychiatrists who diagnosed neurosis and in so doing labelled them as 'psychiatric' cases. They concurred with the diagnoses and the treatment but the label had stigma attached to it and they had to live with the concomitant problems.

A stereotypical happy family consists of husband as breadwinner, wife as mother/housekeeper and a couple of healthy children. Just as men are socialised into accepting that they must work and provide for their families, and feel shame and a sense of inadequacy when they are unable to do so, so women by the same process of socialisation, take responsibility for the health and happiness of the family upon themselves so that the inevitable failures become a source of self-reproach. One answer to failure, real or imagined, is to try harder. Some of the women became obsessional about cleaning, equating uncleanliness with illness; some, caring for elderly or sick members of the family, became so home-centred that they were unable to leave it, becoming agoraphobic. Socialised as they were into acceptance of their roles and beset by exceptionally severe difficulties, the men and women were constrained to find ways of coping within the given situation. The men did not view as realistic the possibility of abandoning a dreary or badly paid job in the hope of finding something better, in the face of widespread unemployment, nor could the women contemplate further education or a career when the demands upon them already seemed overwhelming.

From the sociological perspective, the 'neurotic' individual is the end-product of a particular social constellation (or chain of events) starting with severe problems, leading to the selection of a coping stratagem (influenced by a prevalent social relations) leading on to negotiations with doctors and to labelling by psychiatrists. This perspective is not antagonistic to the possibility of a psychological view of neurosis, indeed it is very likely that psychological as well as social factors govern the perception of problems and the selection of suitable stratagems for coping with them.

Why are women so much more likely than men to develop neurosis, i.e. to become the end products of this chain of events? The answer lies to some extent in the likelihood of women having to contend with more, or more severe, problems for which appropriate coping stratagems have to be found. Work problems are stressful for men but they are no less so for women, whether they confine themselves (or are confined) to housework, or combine domestic duties and paid employment. Women work longer hours than men, without the enjoyment of an end to the day and a period of relaxation. For many women, pre-menstrual tension is a monthly ordeal and the menopause a long drawn-out misery but they are seldom able to relinquish their responsibilities on such grounds. Pregnancy and parturition are necessarily a female function but rearing children and attending to their day-to-day requirements are hardly less automatically the duty of women as is the care of sick and elderly members of the family. Social restraints bear more heavily upon women, leaving them with fewer acceptable stratagems for coping. Men enjoy a freedom of action that is frequently denied to women. General practitioners and psychiatrists may approach their male and female patients differently, often dismissing the problems of the latter as 'women's troubles'. Women are readier to accept the neurotic label than are men, who regard it disparagingly, but this differential only marginally contributes to the preponderance of female neurotics. A far more significant factor is the relative degree of social support enjoyed by men and women; there is evidence that married women receive considerably less emotional support from their husbands than do married men from their wives and that even with regard to practical support, women fare worse. Lack of support compounds problems and renders coping with them that much more difficult.

IMPROVEMENT IN WOMEN

If neurosis is a way of coping with problems, what is the meaning of improvement or recovery? If neurosis is a negotiated agreement between doctor and patient, what do we mean by 'getting better'?

The women of the study were all able to make up their minds, a year after psychiatric referral, whether they were better or not and for most of them the notion of improvement had some clear and specific meaning. They were not asked to rate their improvement or to state whether there was any, they were merely encouraged to talk about changes that had taken place during the year and about present problems. From these conversations it emerged that the women's condition could conveniently be divided into four categories, i.e. worse than a year previously, unchanged, improved, and quite recovered.

Table 7.1: Improvement a year after referral

Respondents' feeling	Women	Men
Quite recovered	14	5
Improved	19	9
Unchanged	20	3
Worse	12	3
Total	65	20

The fourteen women who felt 'recovered' declared themselves to be clear of neurotic problems: 'I am fine, not a trace of depression'; 'I am well, the cloud has lifted' and 'My neurosis is in the past' were just some of the ways in which recovery was expressed. Those who felt that their condition had improved said that they were still experiencing 'ups and downs' although the 'downs' were less severe and less frequent than they were before: one said, 'I am better but still have some bad days' and another, 'The problem is slowly going away . . . I am O.K. during the day but still have trouble sleeping'.

For some, recovery or improvement meant that they could engage in activities which had previously been beyond them: 'I can drive my car alone and I don't mind going over a bridge'; 'I can go to a party and know that I won't start crying' or even more simply, 'I can take the children to school'. To be able to sleep through the night, not to be tearful during the day and no longer to be subject to attacks of panic were other manifestations of getting better, as were coping with housework or the job and getting through the day without feeling exhausted.

Perceptions of improvement were strongly linked to patterns of drug-taking. Of the women in the 'quite recovered' category, twelve had ceased taking any kind of tranquilliser or anti-depressant by the time of the second interviews, the other two had also stopped taking drugs, but kept some in the house by way of 'insurance'.

The women in the 'improved' category were still having one or other psychological drugs prescribed for them although they had struggled to give up, or at least to reduce, their consumption of them. Typical comments were 'I have cut down, the "GP" helps me to take less', and 'I don't take it now, not for the last month or more, but I still collect the repeats [prescriptions], it gives me confidence to have them in the house'. Many women expressed the view that it is easier to curtail or cease drug consumption with the back-up of a supply in the house or a valid prescription.

Sally, 28: 'I feel better now and hardly take any tablets, but I am afraid of getting into a panic if I haven't got any at home. As long as I have the tablets and I know I can take them if I get upset, I feel calm and I manage without them'.

It is interesting that these women felt able to resist taking drugs whilst having them in the house; certainly the experience of alcoholics and smokers is the opposite, that it is better not to have alcohol or cigarettes in the house if you are trying to give up. Possibly the awareness that drugs are available only on prescription is the crucial difference, after all, smokers and drinkers always have the comfort of knowing that supplies are no further away than the corner shop.

Those women who perceived no improvement in their neurotic condition during the year were still relying on drugs. Some had taken them continuously during the year, others had stopped taking them for a while but then resumed, this in spite of the general consensus that drugs did not help in the long run.

What really helped the women who got better?

BENEFICIAL LIFE EVENTS

Of all the factors which proved helpful to the women who reported improvement or recovery, major events of the kind which brought about profound changes in their lives were the most important. These events included divorce or separation, moving house, relief from difficult caring roles and the obtainment of satisfactory employment.

Between the first and second interviews, a period of one year, nine out of the sixty-five women became divorced or were separated from their husbands, a fairly high proportion but hardly surprising considering that the majority of the respondent women saw their marriages as unhappy (see Chapter 1). For these nine women, the change in their marital situation changed their entire lives; all but one of them viewed the end of a troubled marriage as a relief. Four were thankful that a violent husband had departed and 'life could begin again'; four others were glad to be free of a demanding or uncongenial partner or a restrictive marriage. The one exception was a woman whose separation was both a very recent and an exceptionally traumatic experience, who felt confused as to whether, on balance, benefits or damage dominated the situation.

Living without a husband meant that women had to take on the role of main provider, whether by obtaining employment, substituting a full-time for a part-time job or by claiming welfare benefits. Four of the nine women had moved from their marital homes (two returned to their parents) and they all saw changes in their informal networks. Five were having driving lessons or had passed the test, no mean achievement for women so recently diagnosed as psychiatric cases.

Moving to a different house was another beneficial life event. In addition to those just mentioned who left the marital home following divorce, there were eight women who had moved with their families and felt much better as a result. They found themselves living in improved accommodation or in a more congenial neighbourhood which in turn brought other benefits. For example, Lucy had a larger house in a district close to suburban shops. She was also within walking distance of a slimming club (Weightwatchers) where she was not only helped with her weight problem but also found companionship. Likewise Iris, after moving to a bigger house, was able to start her own modest home business. But for some a dry roof or more space was itself a basis for getting better.

Yet another event which aided improvement with neurotic problems was the ending of the role of carer for a sick or disabled relative. This happened to five women who experienced tremendous relief, after initial sadness or grief, on the death or transfer to a residential home of the relatives they had so long cared for.

Finding satisfactory employment lifted neurosis for the very few who were able to achieve it; six women had changed from domestic work only to paid employment or had moved from one paid job to another, resulting variously in greater job satisfaction, the companionship of congenial adults and the confidence that comes from earning money.

In recent years much has been written about stressful life-events, that is, events in people's lives, usually of an adverse and painful nature, which may trigger or even partially cause illness (see Chapter 1). The difficulties of research in this field are numerous and well documented; ideally, events should be studied in relation to the personal meaning they hold for individuals. Even experiences which are assumed to be painful for nearly everyone, such as the death of a much-loved relative, or the loss of a home, are distressing to different people to different degrees; but an in-depth study of the meaning of life events for the individual members of a research sample would be too formidable a task for researchers. In spite of difficulties several attempts have been made to evaluate the significance of various distressing events to the people affected, and scales of life-events have been constructed (Holmes and Rahe, 1967; Paykel, 1974). The scales are based on the assumption that there are certain similarities in the meaning of events to most people and that events can be ranked according to the distress they cause. The scales usually include both externally induced events (death, earthquake) and events brought about by people themselves (suing for divorce, moving house). Life-events have been much investigated in relation to illness causation but little, if any, attention has been paid to the possibility that life-events which to some people are distressing and painful may mean relief and benefit to others. Some time ago Mechanic, a medical sociologist, warned that life-events should not be categorised as wholly pleasant or unpleasant, because most imply a mixture of both. Thus, for example, outwardly positive and favourable events, such as getting married or being promoted, may bring stresses and problems of adjustment (Mechanic, 1968). Nevertheless, the study of stresses and difficulties brought about by events commonly regarded as 'pleasant', and the benefits and the relief that can attend events usually thought of as unpleasant, has been neglected. Divorce or separation from a husband, or the death of a parent, are usually regarded as stressful events of an adverse kind; moving house, also, is for many people a stressful experience. However, in the present study these same events appeared as causal factors in recovery from depression and other neurotic problems.

Thus, most of the women who felt better (whether completely or partially) had experienced events of a kind which brought major changes in the structure of their lives. Indeed, out of thirty-three women whose condition had, by their own reckoning, changed for the better, twenty-five had experienced at least one such event during the year following referral to psychiatrists. It is possible that professional or lay assistance was instrumental in bringing about some of these events, in areas that were open to human volition. Decisions to divorce or separate from husbands, seek employment, move house or place a relative into care may have resulted from discussions with medical or other helping agencies, by a stiffening of resolve following treatment or by having confirmed the 'rightness' of decisions already contemplated. It was clear that in some cases events were induced by the women concerned, in others they 'just happened'.

> *Marjory, 41, three children 15, 18 and 23:* 'Talking to the psychiatrist helped me at the end . . . I decided to leave him [Mick, husband]. The psychiatrist didn't tell me to leave but I could see that he wouldn't blame me for it. Mick made a lot of trouble but my eldest son helped me, he could stand up to his Dad. I am much better now'.

On the other hand Kay, who couldn't bring herself to leave her alcoholic husband, in spite of pressure from her family to do so, found that seven months after she was referred to a psychiatrist her husband announced his intention of obtaining a divorce, and left home. Kay's psychiatric treatment may have had some bearing on the husband's decision to leave but this was hardly likely in the case of Bridget, whose husband left her and the children for another woman, and it was certainly not so in the case of Kim, whose husband was sent to prison. Interestingly, these three women were among those who located their problems, at least partially, in their marriages (see Chapter 1); with the husbands gone, their neurotic condition improved.

Caring roles also came to an end in different ways. For example Jenny, who looked after a schizophrenic mother, took positive steps to obtain residential care for her, following discussions with a counsellor and a self-help group for the relatives of psychiatric patients. May's very demanding task of caring for her paralysed husband ended with his death.

Those who moved house (other than as a consequence of divorce) did not do so as a result of prompting by helpers; they moved because of changes in their husbands' employment, or were rehoused by their local authority. Moreover, some women experienced events of a different kind which they did not initiate themselves but which assisted improvement, among them, a youngest child starting school and a step-daughter passing A-levels and going away to university.

Thus psychiatrists or other professional helpers may have

assisted some women to take decisions that altered their lives; in the case of others, externally induced events changed the structure of existence, creating new situations in which old problems disappeared and neurosis lifted.

WHAT ELSE HELPED?

In the previous chapter, it was said that talking to someone, whether professional or lay helper, was more beneficial than group discussions. The women also singled out as helpful, treatment programmes that constituted a series of limited objectives, each one taking progress a further step forward. For example, Diane's programme, worked out with her psychotherapist, required her first to walk as far as the corner, then to a nearby shop, then to her appointment with the therapist and so on. The usual aim of such programmes is to identify a clear objective which seems manageable. Some of the women adopted such programmes without professional prompting, on the advice of friends or from magazine articles or other reading. Not only those with phobias but also sufferers from depression were helped by 'limited aims' programmes, especially when there was a friend, or self-help group, to whom successes and failures could be reported.

Newly acquired companionship and social support were of the utmost importance for improvement and often derived from one or other of the beneficial changes already noted, such as divorce, moving house or the coming to an end of a caring function. Women so affected were enabled, sometimes indeed forced, to find companionship outside their homes. A new neighbour moving in, an old friend making contact, were examples of occurrences which, by themselves, relieved loneliness and aided improvement. Some women mentioned reading the Bible, taking up yoga, listening to 'soothing' tapes, going on a diet and taking exercise, as things that helped them. Whether the taking up of new activities and the acquisition of new friends followed or preceded improvements in neurosis could not easily be determined. It was argued previously that it is seldom possible to say with any certainty whether, for example, loss of friends or depression came first. Likewise, it is difficult to ascertain whether gaining a friend, losing weight, taking up yoga and so on brought about improvement or resulted from it, and few of the women were interested in analysing the components of the package that constituted improvement.

At the end of the second interviews, women, whether they felt better or not, were asked to look back on their problems and to say what advice they would give to others in a similar position. There was overwhelming agreement on what should not be done: don't take drugs and don't bottle it up. The consensus was that if at all possible, one should find a sympathetic listener with whom to discuss problems. Opinions were divided on whether a professional or lay listener is to be preferred.

LONG-TERM PROBLEMS

What of those who felt no better at all a year after referral? Did they improve later or just go on living with their problems? And how lasting were the gains made by women who perceived themselves to be improved or recovered?

A year after the second interviews, i.e. two years after referral to the psychiatrists, thirty of the women were interviewed for a third time and asked talk to about the past year; Table 7.2 summarises how they felt at the end of that period, compared with a year earlier.

Table 7.2: Improvement in women two years after referral

| Two years after referral n = 30 | One year after referral n = 30 | | | |
	Recovered	Improved	Same	Worse
Recovered (10)	7	2	1	—
Improved since last year (8)	—	3	3	2
Same as last year (10)	—	3	5	2
Worse than last year (2)	—	—	1	1
Total (30)	7	8	10	5

Out of these thirty women, none of the seven who felt completely well and fully recovered after one year had relapsed; in addition three other women had progressed to the point where they too felt recovered. Indeed, the happiest interviews were with these women; they felt that their lives had changed for the better and that the bad times were over.

By the time of the second interviews there were thirty-two women who felt no improvement; fifteen of these were included in the thirty who were interviewed again after two years. Of these, one was among the three mentioned above who felt recovered; six others were able to report improvement.

However, there remained a hard core of sufferers whose condition, whether 'neurosis' or 'unhappiness', appeared not to have improved during the period covered by the research; they seemed to have settled down to living with their problems. A few of these women were eventually admitted for psychiatric treatment (three out of the thirty interviewed for the third time were so admitted; no one had been admitted a year previously). More usual were those whose out-patient psychiatric treatment had been terminated, within the first year or certainly within two, either by psychiatrists who considered nothing was likely to be achieved by further attendance, or by the wish of the patients who felt that continued attendance was pointless or impossible. One said 'I gave up going to the Day Centre, it wasn't doing me any good .. . . I felt more depressed after my sister got a job, she couldn't take me and there is no way I can get there now'.

What follows the termination of psychiatric treatment in these circumstances is return to the general practitioners and, almost certainly, the continuance of drug prescription.

If, as already discussed, beneficial life events and sympathetic assurances aided the women who recovered, or whose condition improved, it might be supposed that the women who found no improvement had been less fortunate in these respects. This, indeed, proved to be the case; out of the thirty-two women in this category at the time of the second interview only three had experienced any event of the kind that had helped others: two had moved to better housing, and the mentally-handicapped son of the third had been taken into hospital. Although the three women concerned regarded these events as 'good' they did not attach particular importance to them because they had firmly located the source of their problems elsewhere. Nor did the two who moved house perceive any ancillary benefits, both had transferred to housing estates which brought their own problems.

Various avenues of help which might have assisted the women who did not improve seemed not to have been utilised by them, or else they had tried and given up. Indeed, the interviews with these women were full of negatives 'I tried but it didn't help' and 'I thought of doing so, but didn't'. Accounts of being discouraged from seeking work, of not being able to join self-help groups and of rejections by the social network, abounded. Understandably, some of the most unhappy women were among those who did not improve.

Surprisingly, not all of such women considered themselves to be unhappy; rather, some were resigned to living with problems that appeared to be static, aided by well-tried, familiar coping mechanisms. For example, at the end of the first year after referral, there were two agoraphobics who felt that they were coping quite well at home and did not want outside interference, while a woman who attributed her depression to the menopause was resigned to having 'ups-and-downs' until the menopause was over, and did not wish to try any of the 'alternative' help sources. 'I am managing all right' and 'best to leave well alone' were typical comments from these settled 'copers'. Indeed, for these women, depression or agoraphobia became a way of coping, a stratagem for managing problems. Moreover, it became a negotiated agreement: negotiated with the doctor and with the family (mainly husband) and agreed as a viable way of life.

IMPROVEMENT IN THE MEN

At first sight it appeared that the men fared rather better than the women: proportionately more of them perceived improvement during the one year following referral to psychiatrists (70 per cent compared to 31 per cent). Those who took sick leave because of neurotic conditions all returned to work; the three men who lost their employment during the year found new jobs quite quickly. Most men thought of improvement in terms of work; those who were not prevented from working by panic attacks or depression, felt 'well enough'.

However, it should be noted that the men found it more difficult to talk about emotional problems and, possibly, to report lack of improvement, than did the women. The men were ashamed to admit to the 'female' condition of neurosis and their feelings of shame intensified during a year of seeing themselves ridiculed and rejected. Inherent in the requirements of masculinity, in a society that regards men as the stronger sex, is that emotional problems are indications of weakness and should be concealed or minimised.

Accordingly, male respondents may have reported improvement through shame and a desire to seem manly, especially when facing a woman researcher. Saying 'all is well now' also has the benefit of reducing interview time: certainly the second interviews with the men were shorter and brisker than the first.

If improvement was genuinely greater for men, it could be because they received a higher level of marital support and because more effort was made by the psychiatrists and others to whom they turned for help. Interestingly, the men did not experience life-events to anything like the same extent as did the women who showed improvement: none of them were divorced or separated and only one moved house during the year; there were no major work-related changes.

THE WAY FORWARD

This research did not set out to test the efficacy of psychiatric treatment for conditions termed 'neurotic' nor is such a test within the purview of sociology. However, from their own testimony, no fewer than twenty-five out of the thirty-three women who improved or recovered within a year of psychiatric referral attributed their progress to beneficial life-events and their side-effects. Conversely, among the women who reported no improvement, beneficial life-events were almost entirely absent.

In some cases, beneficial life-events were fortuitous; others were brought about by respondents' own volition. In these latter instances, the possibility must be allowed that improvements in their neurotic condition preceded the taking of vital decisions by patients which changed their lives. But various agencies helped with improvement and psychiatrists were no better rated in this respect, by the female respondents, than were other helpers.

The evidence of this research is that neurosis is a social disorder lending itself to social remedies. It would appear that psychiatric skills are inappropriate to the treatment of neurosis and that those general practitioners who describe neurotic symptoms as 'women's troubles' are right, even if for the wrong reason. If neurosis is another word for unhappiness, its medicalisation is unlikely to prove beneficial. However, people do take their troubles to the doctor, and the attachment of other helpers to surgeries may well point the way forward.

References

Ablon, J. (1981) 'Stigmatised health conditions', *Social Science and Medicine,* 15B, 5–9.

Baldwin, S. and Glendenning, C. (1983) 'Employment, women and their disabled children', in Finch, J. and Groves, D. (eds), *A Labour of Love,* London: Routledge and Kegan Paul.

Balint, M. (1957) *The Doctor, His Patient and the Illness.* Second edition 1964, London: Pitman.

Barrett, M. (1979) *Virginia Woolf: Women and Writing,* London: The Women's press.

Barrett, M. and Roberts, H. (1978) 'Doctors and their patients: the social control of women in general practice', in Smart, C. and Smart, B. (eds), *Women, Sexuality and Social Control,* London: Routledge and Kegan Paul.

Baruch, G. and Treacher, A. (1978) *Psychiatry Observed,* London: Routledge and Kegan Paul.

Becker, G. (1981) 'Coping with stigma: lifelong adaptation of deaf people', *Social Science and Medicine,* 15B, 21–4.

Becker, H.S. (1963) *Outsiders,* New York: Free press.

Birenbaum, A. (1970) 'On managing a courtesy stigma', *Journal of Health and Social Behaviour,* 11, 196–206.

Blaxter, M. (1976) *The Meaning of Disability,* London: Heinemann.

Blaxter, M. (1978) 'Diagnosis as category and process: the case of alcoholism', *Social Science and Medicine,* 12, 9–17.

Blaxter, M. and Patterson, E. (1982) *Mothers and Daughters: A Three-generational Study of Health Attitudes and Behaviour,* London: Heinemann.

Bloom, J.R. (1982) 'Social support, accommodation to stress and adjustment to breast cancer', *Social Science and Medicine,* 16, 1329–38.

Bott, E. (1957) *Family and Social Network,* London: Tavistock.

Brockman, J., D'Arcy, C. and Edmonds, L. (1979) 'Facts or artifacts?

Changing public attitudes towards the mentally ill', *Social Science and Medicine,* 13A, 673–82.

Brown, A.T. (1986) 'Coping with Agoraphobia', Ph.D. thesis, University of Southampton.

Brown, G.W. (1984) 'Depression: a sociological view', in Black, N. *et al.* (eds), *Health and Disease,* Milton Keynes: Open University Press.

Brown, G.W., Davidson, S., Harris, T., MacLean, U. and Prudo, R. (1977) 'Psychiatric disorder in London and North Uist', *Social Science and Medicine,* 11, 367–77.

Brown, G.W. and Harris, T. (1978) *Social Origins of Depression,* London: Tavistock.

Byrne, P.S. and Long, B.E. (1976) *Doctors Talking to Patients,* London: HMSO.

Cartwright, A. (1967) *Patients and their Doctors,* London: Routledge and Kegan Paul.

Cartwright, A. (1970) *Life Before Death,* London: Routledge and Kegan Paul.

Cartwright, A. and Anderson, R. (1981) *General Practice Revisited,* London: Tavistock.

Chavkin, W. (1981) *Double Exposure,* New York: Monthly Review Press.

Chetwynd, J. and Hartnett, O. (1978) (eds), *The Sex Role System,* London: Routledge and Kegan Paul.

Choiton, A., Spitzer, W.O., Roberts, S.R. and Delmore T. (1976) 'The patterns of medical drug use', *Canadian Medical Association Journal,* 114, 33.

Clare, A. and Lader, M. (1982) *Psychiatry and General Practice,* London: Academic Press.

Cooperstock, R. (1978) 'Sex difference is psychotropic drug use', *Social Science and Medicine,* 12, 3B, 179–86.

Cooperstock, R. and Lennard, H. (1979) 'Some social meanings of tranquillizer use', *Sociology of Health and Illness,* 1, 3, 33.

Cooperstock, R. and Parnell, P. (1982) 'Research on psychotropic drug use', *Social Science and Medicine,* 16, 1179–96.

Crocetti, G., Spiro, H.R. and Siass, I. (1974) *Contemporary Attitudes Towards Mental Illness,* Pittsburgh: Pittsburgh University Press.

Cumming, E. and Cumming, J. (1957) *Closed Ranks,* Cambridge, Mass: Harvard University Press.

D'Arcy, C. and Brockman, J. (1976) 'Changing public recognition of psychiatric symptoms?', *Journal of Health and Social Behaviour,*

17, 302–10.

D'Arcy, C. and Brockman, J. (1977) 'Public rejection of the ex-mental patients: are attitudes changing?', *Canadian Review of Sociology and Anthropology,* 14, 68–80.

Davis, F. (1963) *Passage Through Crisis,* New York: Bobbs-Merrill.

Davis, F. (1964) 'Deviance disavowal: the management of strained interaction by the visibly handicapped', in Becker, H.S. (ed.), *The Other Side,* New York: Free Press.

DHSS (1983) *Mental Illness: Policies for Prevention, Treatment, Rehabilitation and Care,* London: HMSO.

Doll, W., Thompson, E. and Lefton, M. (1976) 'Beneath acceptance', *Social Science and Medicine,* 10, 312–17.

Doyal, L. (1979) The Political Economy of Health, London: Pluto Press.

Edgerton, R. (1967) *The Cloak of Competence: Stigma in the Lives of the Mentally Retarded,* Berkeley: University of California Press.

Evason, E. (1980) *Just Me and the Kids: a Study of Single-parent Families,* Belfast: Equal Opportunities Commission.

Evers, H. (1985) 'The frail elderly woman: emerging questions in ageing and women's health', in Lewin, E. and Olesen, V. (eds), *Women, Health and Healing,* London: Tavistock.

Field, D. (1976) 'The social definition of illness', in Tuckett, D. (ed.), *An Introduction to Medical Sociology,* London: Tavistock.

Finch, J. and Groves, C. (1983) *A Labour of Love: Women, Work and Caring,* London: Routledge and Kegan Paul.

Finkelstein, V. (1980) *Attitudes and Disabled People,* New York: World Rehabilitation Fund.

Fransella, A. and Frost, K. (1977) *How Women See Themselves,* London: Tavistock.

Freidson, E. (1970) *Profession of Medicine,* New York: Dodd Mead.

Friedan, B. (1963) *The Feminine Mystique,* London: Gallancz.

Funch, D.P. and Mettlin, C. (1982) 'The role of social support in relation to recovery from breast surgery', *Social Science and Medicine,* 16, 91–8.

Gallagher, E.B. (1976) 'Lines of reconstruction and extensions in the Parsonian sociology of illness', *Social Science and Medicine,* 10, 207–18.

Garmanikov, E., Morgan, D., Purvis, J. and Taylorson, D. (1983A) (eds), *The Public and the Private,* London: Heinemann.

Garmanikov, E., Morgan, D., Purvis, J. and Taylorson, D. (1983B)

Gender, Class and Work, London: Heinemann.

Gavron, H. (1966) *The Captive Wife,* London: Routledge and Kegan Paul.

Goffman, E. (1961) *Asylums,* New York: Doubleday; 1968, Harmondsworth, Middlesex: Penguin Books.

Goldberg, D. and Huxley, P. (1980) *Mental Illness in the Community,* London: Tavistock.

Grad, J. and Sainsbury, P. (1968) 'The effects that patients have on their families in a community care and a control psychiatric service', *British Journal of Psychiatry,* 114, 265.

Graham, H. (1983) 'Caring: a labour of love', in Finch, J. and Groves, C. (eds), *A Labour of Love,* London: Routledge and Kegan Paul.

Graham, H. (1984) *Women, Health and the Family,* Brighton, Sussex: Wheatsheaf Books.

Hanmer, J. and Saunders, S. (1983) 'Blowing the cover of the protective male: a community study of violence to women', in Garmanikov, E., Morgan, D., Purvis, J. and Taylorson, D. (eds), *The Public and the Private,* London: Heinemann.

Harrison, P. (1983) *Inside the Inner City: Life Under the Cutting Edge,* Harmondsworth, Middlesex: Penguin Books.

Hart, N. (1976) *When Marriage Ends,* London: Tavistock.

Hemminki, E. (1974) 'General practitioners' indications for psychotropic drug therapy', *Scandinavian Journal of Social Medicine,* 2, 1.

Hemminki, E., Pesonen, T. and Bruun, K. (1981) 'Sales of psychotropic drugs in the Nordic countries', *Social Science and Medicine,* 15A, 589–99.

Henderson, S., Byrne, D.C., Duncan-Jones, P., Adcock, S., Scott, R. and Steele, G.P. (1978) 'Social bonds in the epidemiology of neurosis', *British Journal of Psychiatry,* 133, 106.

Higgins, P.C. (1980) *Outsiders in a Hearing World,* London: Russell Sage.

Hobson, D. (1978) 'Housewives: isolation as oppression', in Women's Studies Group, University of Birmingham (ed.), *Women Take Issue: Aspects of Women's Subordination,* London: Hutchinson.

Holmes, T.H. and Rahe, R.H. (1967) 'The social readjustment rating scale', *Journal of Psychosomatic Research,* 11, 213–18.

Hopper, S. (1981) 'Diabetes as a stigmatised condition', *Social Science and Medicine,* 15B, 11–19.

Jefferys, M. and Sachs, H. (1983) *Rethinking General Practice,* London: Tavistock.

Jerrome, D. (1981) 'The significance of friendship for women in later life', *Ageing and Society,* 1, 175–97.

Kadushin, C. (1969) *Why People Go to Psychiatrists,* New York: Atherton.

Klerman, G.L., (1978) 'Stress, adaptation and affective disorders'. Paper presented to the American Psychopathological Association, March, Boston.

Knudson-Cooper, M. (1981) 'Adjustment to visible stigma', *Social Science and Medicine,* 15B, 31–44.

Komarovsky, M. (1967) *Blue Collar Marriage,* New York: Vintage Books.

Koumjian, K. (1981) 'The use of Valium as a form of social control', *Social Science and Medicine,* 15E, 245.

Land, H. (1983) 'Poverty and gender: the distribution of resources within the family', in M. Brown (ed.) *The Structure of Disadvantage,* London: Heinemann.

Leeson, J. and Gray, J. (1978) *Women and Medicine,* London: Tavistock.

Lemert, E. (1951) *Social Pathology,* New York: McGraw-Hill.

Litman, G.K. (1978) 'Clinical aspects of sex-role stereotyping', in Chetwynd, J. and Hartnett, O. (eds), *The Sex Role System,* London: Routledge and Kegan Paul.

Littlewood, R. and Lipsedge, M. (1982) *Aliens and Alienists,* Harmondsworth, Middlesex: Penguin Books.

Lynam, J. (1985) 'Support network developed by immigrant women', *Social Science and Medicine,* 21, 3.

May, A. and Gregory, E. (1968) 'Participation of general practitioners in psychiatry', *British Medical Journal,* 2, 168–71.

McKee, L. (1983) 'Wives and the recession'. Paper presented to the Conference on Unemployment and its Effects on the Family, University of Birmingham.

Mechanic, D. (1968) *Medical Sociology,* New York: Free Press.

Meile, R. and Whitt, H. (1981) 'Cultural consensus and definition of mental illness', *Social Science and Medicine,* 15A, 231–42.

Miles, A. (1977) 'Staff relations in psychiatric hospitals', *British Journal of Psychiatry,* 130, 84–8.

Miles, A. (1978) 'The social content of health', in Brearley, P., Gibbons, J., Miles, A. and Topliss, E. (eds) *The Social Context of Health Care,* Oxford: Martin Robertson.

Miles, A. (1979) 'Some psycho-social consequences of multiple sclerosis: a study of group identity', *British Journal of Medical Psychology*, 52, 321–31.

Miles, A. (1984) 'The stigma of psychiatric disorder: a sociological perspective and research report', in Reed, J. and Lomas, G. (eds), *Psychiatric Services in the Community*, London: Croom Helm.

Miles, A. (1987) *The Mentally Ill in Contemporary Society*, Oxford: Blackwell.

Millum, T. (1975) *Images of Women: Advertising in Women's Magazines*, London: Chatto and Windus.

Mishler, E.G. (1981) 'The social construction of illness', in Mishler, E.G. (ed.), *The Social Context of Health, Illness and Patient Care*, Cambridge: Cambridge University Press.

Nicholson, P. (1986) 'Developing a feminist approach to depression following childbirth', in Wilkinson, S. (ed.), *Feminist Social Psychology*, Milton Keynes, Bucks: Open University Press.

Oakley,A. (1974) *The Sociology of Housework*, Oxford: Martin Robertson.

Oakley, A. (1981A) 'Interviewing women: A contradiction in terms', in Roberts, H., *Doing Feminist Research*, London: Routledge and Kegan Paul.

Oakley, A. (1981B) *Subject Women*, Oxford: Martin Robertson.

OHE (Office of Health Economics) (1975) *Medicines Which Affect the Mind*, London: OHE.

Parlee, M.B. (1976) 'The premenstrual syndrome', in Cox, S. (ed.), *Female Psychology: Emerging Self*, Chicago: Science Research Associates.

Parsons, T. (1951) *The Social System*, London: Free Press.

Parsons, T. (1958) 'Definitions of health and illness in the light of American values and social structure', in Jaco, E.G. (ed.), *Patients, Physicians and Illness*, New York: Free Press.

Paykel, E.S. (1974) 'Recent life events and clinical depression', in Gundersen, E.K.E. and Rahe, R.D. (eds), *Life Stress and Illness*, Illinois: Charles Thomas.

Penfold, S. and Walker, G. (1984) *Women and the Psychiatric Paradox*, Milton Keynes: Open University Press.

Phillips, D.L. (1966) 'Public identification and acceptance of the mentally ill', *American Journal of Public Health*, 56, 755–63.

Pilisuk, M. and Froland, C. (1978) 'Kinship, social networks, social support and health', *Social Science and Medicine*, 12B, 273–80.

Richman, A. and Barry, A. (1985) 'More and more is less and less: the myth of massive psychiatric need', *British Journal of Psychiatry,* 146, 164.

Roberts, H. (1985) *The Patient Patients,* London: Pandora.

Roberts, H. (1981A) 'Women and their doctors', in Roberts, H. (ed.), *Doing Feminist Research,* London: Routledge and Kegan Paul.

Roberts, H. (1981B) *Women, Health and Reproduction,* London: Routledge and Kegan Paul.

Robinson, D. (1971) *The Process of Becoming Ill,* London: Routledge and Kegan Paul.

Rosenberg, M.G. (1984) 'The home is the workplace', in Chavkin, W. (ed.), *Double Exposure,* New York: Monthly Review Press.

Rosenhan, D.L. (1973) 'On being sane in insane places', *Science,* 179, 250–8.

Row, D. (1983) *Depression,* London: Routledge and Kegan Paul.

Rubin, L.B. (1976) *Worlds of Pain: Life in the Working Class Family,* New York: Basic Books.

Sampson, H., Messinger, S.L. and Towne, R.D. (1968) 'Family processes and becoming a mental patient', in Spitzer, S.P. and Denzin, N.K. (eds), *The Mental Patient,* New York: McGraw-Hill.

Sarsby, J. (1972) 'Love and marriage', *New Society,* 28 September.

Scheff, T.J. (1966) *Being Mentally Ill,* Chicago: Aldine.

Schur, E.M. (1980) *The Politics of Deviance,* New Jersey: Prentice Hall.

Scott, R.A. (1969) *The Making of the Blind Men,* London: Russell Sage.

Sharpe, S. (1984) *Double Identity,* Harmondsworth, Middlesex: Penguin Books.

Shearer, A. (1981) *Disability: Whose Handicap?* Oxford: Blackwell.

Shepherd, M., Cooper, B., Brown, A.C. and Kalton, G.W. (1966) *Psychiatric Illness in General Practice,* London: London University Press.

Smith, D. and David, S. (1975) *Women Look at Psychiatry,* New York: Press Gang.

Stanton, A.H. and Schwarz, M.S. (1954) *The Mental Hospital,* New York: Basic Books.

Stimson, G. (1976) 'General Practitioners, trouble and types of patients', in Stacey, M. (ed.), *The Sociology of the NHS,* Keele: Keele University Press.

Stimson, G. and Webb, B. (1975) *Going to See the Doctor,* London: Routledge and Kegan Paul.

Trefgarne (1984) 'Developments in community psychiatry: a central view', in Reed, J. and Lomas, G. (eds), *Psychiatric Services in the Community,* London: Croom Helm.

Ungerson, C. (1983) 'Women and caring: skills, tasks and taboos', in Garmanikov, E., Morgan, D., Purvis, J. and Taylorson, D. (eds), *The Public and the Private,* London: Heinemann.

Vaughn, C.E. and Leff, J.P. (1976) 'The influence of family and social factors on the course of psychiatric illness', *British Journal of Psychiatry,* 129, 125–37.
Venters, M. (1981) 'Familial coping with chronic and severe childhood illness'. *Social Science and Medicine,* 15A, 289–97.
Verbrugge, L. (1984) 'How physicians treat mentally distressed men and women', *Social Science and Medicine,* 18, 1.
Voysey, M. (1975) *A Constant Burden,* London: Routledge and Kegan Paul.

Wadsworth, M., Butterfield, W.J. and Blaney, R. (1971) *Health and Sickness: the Choice of Treatment,* London: Tavistock.
Waldron, I. (1977) 'Increased prescribing of Valium, Librium and other drugs', *International Journal of Health Services,* 7, 41.
Waldron, I. (1982) 'Cross cultural variations in blood pressure', *Social Science and Medicine,* 16, 419–30.
Weidegar, P. (1978) *Female Cycles,* London: The Women's Press.
Weissman, M. and Klerman, G.L. (1977) 'Sex differences and the epidemiology of depression', *Archives of General Psychiatry,* 24, 98–111.
Weissman, M. and Paykel, E.S. (1974) *The Depressed Woman,* Chicago: University of Chicago Press.
Wilkinson, S. (1986) 'Sighting possibilities, diversity and commonality in feminist research', in Wilkinson, S. (ed.) *Feminist Social Psychology,* Milton Keynes: Open University Press.
Wood, G. (1983) *The Myth of Neurosis,* London: Macmillan.
Wyeth (1980) *Glossary of Mental Disorders,* Maidenhead, Berkshire: Wyeth Laboratories.

Young, G. (1981) 'A woman in medicine—reflections from the inside', in Roberts, H. (ed.), *Women, Health and Reproduction,* London: Routledge and Kegan Paul.
Young, M. and Willmott, P. (1962) *Family and Kinship in East London,* Harmondsworth, Middlesex: Penguin Books.

Zola, I.K. (1972) 'Medicine as an institution of social control', *Sociological Review,* 20, 4, 487.

Zola, I.K. (1973) 'Pathways to the doctor: from person to patient', *Social Science and Medicine,* 7, 677–89.

Index